CEDAR PARK PUBLIC LIBRARY
5 4161 00169626 4

D0561340

Confessions *from the* Corner Office

15 Instincts That Will Help You Get There

Confessions *from the* Corner Office

15 Instincts That Will Help You Get There

Scott Aylward and Pattye Moore

John Wiley & Sons, Inc.

Published by John Wiley & Sons, Inc., Hoboken, New Jersey.
Published simultaneously in Canada.

Wiley Bicentennial Logo: Richard J. Pacifico

For general information on our other products and services or for technical support, please contact our Customer Care Department within the United States at (800) 762-2974, outside the United States at (317) 572-3993 or fax (317) 572-4002.

Wiley also publishes its books in a variety of electronic formats. Some content that appears in print may not be available in electronic books. For more information about Wiley products, visit our web site at www.wiley.com.

ISBN-13: 978-0-470-12678-3

Printed in the United States of America.

10 9 8 7 6 5 4 3 2 1

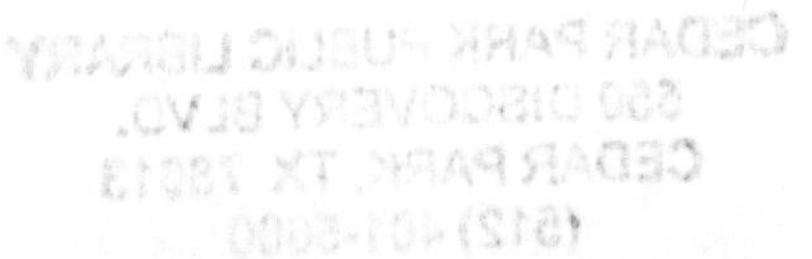

Contents

Preface

A Promise. A Secret. An Instinct.

Pattye: Don't you think we're being a bit dramatic with the title for our introduction? This is a book on management and leadership, not "Days of Our Lives."

Scott: Actually, Pattye, you're wrong. (I wonder if I'll get to say that a lot in this book.) It is a book on leadership, but it is also a book on the Days of OUR Lives. Since we're sharing what we've learned over the years, you can't really separate the two.

Pattye: Let me clear up one thing right away. No, you will not get to say "you're wrong" a lot in this book. I can see in your face that it provided you way too much joy just to say it that first time.

Scott: I sort of figured that. But our past and how we started our careers all comes into play as to how we developed our leadership and management philosophies. I think most who are successful in business can point to a person, an event, or a reason that influenced their drive for corporate success.

Pattye: I think it is safe to say that each of us had a defining moment or event that caused us to shift gears into overdrive when it came to our careers. And once we shifted, we had no choice but to develop the leadership and management instincts that we share in this book.

Scott: Well, we had a choice; everyone has a choice.

Pattye: Not if we wanted to get to the corner office, we didn't.

Scott: Point taken, Madame President. You know, it might have been nice to downshift on occasion, say, once every four or five years—but hey, no sense crying over spilled milk. I think we should start this business book by sharing with the reader what it was that ignited you and me with an unrelenting drive and passion to make it to the top, and to get there on our own terms and, more importantly, with our integrity fully intact.

Pattye: Okay, I'll share, but just this one time. Then it's on to the instincts and no more looking back. Okay, Mr. Nostalgia? For me, it was a promise.

Scott: Sounds to me like we have the makings of a Lifetime made for TV movie. For me, it was a secret. Talk about luck! That is exactly what we named this Preface. By the way, if I haven't told you, I feel so lucky to have met you midway in my career. What are the odds of crossing paths with someone who shares your instincts and in turn becomes your corporate soul mate? I just want you to know I feel lucky.

Pattye: Why lucky?

Scott: Because then I only had to write half the book! Enough about that—let's tell our readers where we got our inspiration and drive.

Pattye's Story

My story starts in 1985. It seemed to be an ordinary, hectic morning in Tulsa, Oklahoma, just like every day, as I juggled my job as an account executive at an ad agency with the demands of being a wife and mother. I remember being quite nervous that particular day because of a big presentation I was making later that morning—in fact, the biggest presentation of my career. Also, I had just made the decision to spend more time with my 1½-year-old daughter by taking the part-time job a friend had offered me at his public relations agency. I was getting ready to walk out the door when my husband of six years came into the kitchen and told me we needed to talk—and no, it couldn't wait. He announced that he had met someone else and wanted a divorce and that he was moving out immediately.

To say that this was shocking and unexpected news would be the understatement of the decade. There had been no visible signs of marital problems, no arguments, no separation, no counseling—no warning. In an instant and without warning, I suddenly became the mommy and daddy, chief bottle washer, and sole breadwinner. I was consumed with fear and uncertainty, but falling apart was not an option at the moment. I stuffed the shock and emotions in my pocket, went to work, and proceeded to make the presentation that morning. Then, I came home and cried.

At that moment, I made a decision and a silent promise to my daughter. I would do whatever it took to provide the life for Melissa that I had envisioned. I had absolutely no idea how, but I was determined to find out. Armed with my new decision and lots of resolve, I did two things. First, I told my friend that I couldn't take the part-time job, and then, I told my boss at the ad agency that I needed to know what I had to do to get promoted and make more money.

Little did I know that years later that silent promise would propel me to the corner office of a major restaurant chain and allow me to carry a business card (yes, my business card) that read "President."

Scott's Story

It was 1980. I was in Houston, Texas, and I wanted only one thing for my life, to have a successful career in advertising. Ever since I took the Introduction to Advertising class as a freshman at Michigan State University, it was THE dream I had for my life after college.

As luck would have it, after a waiter stint, a one-day job with a construction crew, and a failed attempt for an in-house jewelry ad department, I had finally landed in the place I had always dreamed of—a real live advertising agency.

A year earlier I had informed the University and my parents that I was going to leave the graduate program and start my career in Houston, Texas. A high school friend had moved there and offered me a closet for my clothes and a floor to sleep on. This was all the incentive I needed. I packed up my Pinto and off I went to test myself and start my career in advertising, rather than learn about a potential career in advertising.

As I look back now, the move was about self-survival, self-discovery, and learning how to cope with my deepest secret which I had yet to reveal to anyone but myself.

Somewhere during my first six months on the job, "it" happened. I found myself at a golf outing with clients and as the round progressed, the jokes became more off-color. It had reached the point where I was forcing myself to laugh at the latest AIDS joke and other gay-lifestyle-related quips. You see, the jokes were not funny to me.

I was a gay man, but those words were never spoken to family, friends, or even to myself until that day.

Here I was on the verge of living my professional dream and I was doing it while living in constant fear that, if it became known I was gay, it would be easy for management to pass me by. True or not, this was the world I had created. Remember it was 1980, I was 21, and in Texas. I spent as much time and energy guarding my secret as I did on the work I was hired to do. It was overwhelming and exhausting. I played the game I thought I needed to play in order to be trusted, respected, and promoted—a game that required me to carefully select my words when asked what I did over the weekend, and with whom. I did this in order to be liked, yet with each forced laugh I felt myself die a little inside.

On the drive home from golf that day, I can remember being consumed by anger, not at my colleagues, but at myself. Rather than accepting myself and focusing my energy on the start of a successful career, I spent my time hiding and covering up the fear of being found out. This anger turned to a realization that I could not live the rest of my life worried about being successful at hiding something. I wanted, and I needed, to live the rest of my life standing for something successful. And that something would be exceptional performance in my chosen profession.

It was during that drive home after golf and later at home that night that I committed myself to becoming successful as myself, focusing my energy on being an overachiever. I realized that to fulfill my dream of a fast-rising advertising career, I had to work harder and smarter in order to neutralize the potential for being the victim of some misguided prejudice.

I began to display a visible passion for the business and my clients. From that point on, I became driven in my chosen profession. I knew that creative success together with financial results was the way to build a successful career with a path to the corner office. On a more personal note, I realized that, as I became more successful in business, the easier it would be for me to open up to my parents. It was my game plan from that night on to provide them with a sense of pride in *me* and what *I* had accomplished in order to make opening up to them easier.

As I look back, I realize that those hurtful jokes on the golf course motivated me to prove to myself and my colleagues that success is an internal decision, a choice. I was forced to look at the future, and take a gut check. I asked and answered the question "At what level must I perform to achieve my dream of success so that the fear of professional bias goes away?"

Little did I know that having confidence in myself personally and professionally would allow me to proudly carry a business card (yes, my business card!) that read "President," then "CEO," of the largest employee-owned advertising agency in the country.

Scott and Pattye's Story

Early in both of our careers (when we didn't know each other), we realized that we needed an edge to become the kind of leaders others would want to follow. Our insatiable drive to find this edge and to succeed was driven quite simply by the obsession to succeed—although for very different reasons. With this edge, I (Pattye) could keep the promise I made to my daughter. And I (Scott) could use this drive, this edge, to build loyalty and results so strong that my secret would be labeled insignificant. My dream career in advertising would be safe and my parents would speak of my accomplishments—and of me—with pride.

The motivation to succeed based on standing out among our peers caused each of us to develop a series of management instincts. These instincts weren't anything either of us was taught in school. Instead, they came from on-the-job experience and the careful observation of successful leaders around us. These instincts still govern both of us on a daily basis and determine how we treat others and our expectations of ourselves. Unbeknownst to both of us, we individually developed the same group of management instincts as we rose quickly up the corporate ladder. And, we still had yet to hear of each other—our corporate soul mate. Ironically, when we did finally meet professionally, *we recognized the fear, the drive, and the instincts in each other, and we were drawn to support and help each other.*

Becoming Corporate Soul Mates

Pattye: After my divorce, I focused on building a new life. By 1994, I was remarried to a wonderful man, had a second daughter, and was vice president of marketing for Sonic Corp., one of the fastest growing fast-food restaurant chains in the country.

Scott: During that time, I kept moving up the corporate ladder by taking different jobs with different agencies. I moved from Minneapolis to Dallas, back to Minneapolis, on to Detroit, Los Angeles, San Diego, Columbus, then back to where it all began with my first agency in Houston. As I look back, it's amazing that the person who had never moved anywhere until the age of 21, would move eight times in seven years! But, by this point, my parents not only embraced me as a successful advertising professional but also as a son who happened to be gay.

Then came that fateful day. Pattye had decided that Sonic had outgrown the capabilities of their current agency and needed to conduct an agency review. This was a gut-wrenching decision for Pattye, but as you continue to read our book, you will see that one of the instincts we both developed was to always be objective when evaluating talent—regardless of the personal relationship that had been formed with that talent.

At the time of Pattye's decision, I was working at an ad agency in Houston. The agency had lost a large restaurant client and was aggressively attempting to land another client in that same category. Sonic heard our agency was available so they sent us a request for proposal to bid on handling their advertising account. I was selected to head up the pitch. As a result, this took me to Oklahoma City on several occasions to meet with Sonic's marketing group. I met this lady, Pattye, and was blown away. I had never seen anyone who was so together and so genuine. Marketing people in general are a bit full of themselves; however, she was the real deal. I remember being impressed that she terminated her old agency (with whom she had worked for eight years), knowing it would probably cause them to close their doors. To this day, that was one of the most impressive decisions for a 34-year-old professional to make. While it was undoubtedly the right thing to do, it could not have been easy.

Pattye: I remember the first time I met Scott. I knew immediately that we were kindred spirits and that we could work well together. He was the smartest fast-food marketer I had ever met and was fun to work with. But more than that, he had this drive that I recognized quite well—it was the same drive that had landed me here. I wanted him to work on the Sonic business, but it wasn't meant to be. Although Scott was impressive, our review team didn't select his agency. I had promised the agencies an answer that day, but the call to Scott was one call I didn't want to make. I knew how badly he wanted to work with us, and hearing him attempt to sound unmoved and professional on the other end of the line was painful.

Scott: There was no contact—not even a word spoken between us after that day—for over a year. Then the phone rang in my office in Houston one day. The agency that had won the Sonic campaign a year earlier was on the other end of the line asking me if I would like to become the lead on the Sonic account.

I confirmed that Pattye Moore was still vice president of marketing and within weeks I was on my way to an agency in Kansas City, Missouri. I had never been to Kansas City before, but geography was of little importance to me. For the first time in my life, I took a job based, not on the accounts I would be working on, but rather on a gut instinct to work with someone whom, I admit, I barely knew, but who, nonetheless, was someone I already believed in.

Little did I know that weeks earlier, prior to the call to ask me about the job, the agency was informed that Sonic was unhappy with their team leader. In the not-too-distant future, Sonic would become a $100 million advertiser and wanted a strong leader at the top. Pattye told me she suggested they might want to check out this guy named Scott who pitched the business for another agency a year before, though she was not sure if I even still lived in Houston!

Scott and Pattye's Story

So, in 1994, we began our unique partnership. We traveled together for work, spent days driving and shopping the competition from market to market, and were on the phone constantly challenging each other about what made sense for the brand. We discovered we had a similar work ethic and passion for the business. And we loved using each other as a sounding board in the hopes of creating a better idea. We also found that we had developed similar instincts about working with people.

We knew that our corporate relationship was unique, but we didn't often discuss it. In time, we began to hear others talking about the unique business synergy that the two of us had and quite honestly, it was reaffirming to hear that others recognized our partnership and management style. We were told that others knew that, if the two of us were together for a period of time, some initiative would be brought forth, or some brand-defining question would need to be answered.

We didn't know it then but one of the instincts we both had developed was what we now call "finding a corporate soul mate." We had truly become soul mates—corporate soul mates.

We believe that instinct, coupled with the others we developed and nurtured, helped to fuel record growth at our respective companies. Barkley Evergreen and Partners (Scott's advertising agency) more than doubled in size and developed a new, nationwide client list. The agency was recognized as one of the fastest-growing in the country as well as the largest employee-owned agency.

In the years we worked together, Sonic grew from less than $900 million to just over $3 billion in systemwide sales; store-level volumes and profits more than doubled; and Sonic was consistently ranked by *Forbes* and other business publications as one of the best franchising opportunities and fastest-growing companies in the United States.

These instincts also helped fuel our individual careers as well. When we met in 1994, we were both vice presidents. But as one of us moved up the corporate ladder, it wasn't long before the other one moved up as well. We like to say we were pushing and pulling each other up (and we truly were!). And, before we knew it, we had both reached the corner office (Scott as chairman/CEO of Barkley Evergreen and Partners and Pattye as president of Sonic Corp.).

Never in our wildest dreams did either of us believe we would ever make it to the corner office. But we did and so can you.

We believe that there were 15 critical management instincts that we developed and practiced that helped us get there. That's why we're sharing what we call the Essential Corner Office Instincts with you. Develop, nurture, practice, and hone these 15 Corner Office Instincts, and you will be more valued by those you work for and more loved by those who work for you. And, you too can make it to the corner office.

—Scott and Pattye

Acknowledgments

We would like to offer special thanks to:

Dorcas Meroney: Where would we and this book be without you? You have been a great friend to both of us for over 12 years. Thank you for your guidance, inspiration, and for helping us stay on track and focused.

Laverne and Francisco Ríos (Pattye's sister and brother-in-law): Thank you for being our copy and style editors. You literally brought the book home, and it's in a much better place because of you. Plus, Laverne, you're a pretty awesome big sis who has always been there for me (Pattye).

Laurie Harting (our editor at Wiley): Thanks for taking a chance on us and for helping us find our "voice."

We are very fortunate because there were many great leaders, mentors, and friends who shared and shaped our journey. They influenced us in ways that literally strengthened and nourished our souls, touched our hearts, and helped us grow as leaders and as human beings.

To Craig Abbott, Chuck Harrison, Jack Hartnett, Dick Lear, and Bobby Merritt: Special thanks to each of you. You showed us how to lead from the heart, and you changed our lives forever.

To all the Sonic franchisees and operators: You fueled our passion for the business, taught us so many leadership lessons, and made the journey fun and exciting. Thank you.

To Bill Fromm and Cliff Hudson: Thank you for allowing us the freedom to stretch and to become our own brand of leaders.

To Kevin McMillan, Charles Halliburton (AVCOM Productions), and Karri Hartman: Thank you for sharing your creative energy and talents to help us polish our image and get ready for our next adventure.

From Scott

Thank you, Mom and Dad, for giving me unconditional support as well as an entire page in your address book as I moved around the country. Your integrity, humor, and love are a large part of me.

To Ms. McFarline, my high school forensics teacher at Edsel Ford High School, who taught me the power of delivering the spoken word.

To Art Casper for giving me my first job in advertising and rescuing me from the graveyard shift I was working as a waiter.

To Bill Fogarty, an owner of Fogarty/Klein in Houston, who taught me that you can run a business with style and ethics.

To Sue Harwell, my client at Pizza Hut, who showed me that you can motivate people and treat them with respect, fairness, and dignity.

A very special thanks to Lisa Chase for managing my time and my life and for taking care of me for so many years. You allowed me the freedom to do what I do best, and to not miss a beat at running the agency.

To Tom Millweard for an incredible journey and partnership! I could not have made my mark without you by my side as my partner and friend. We were intent on reinventing the agency in a way we could both be proud of and we did. Thank you, Tom, for making my tenure of leading the agency both enjoyable and rewarding. You never allowed me to get too down, and I can't tell you how much I appreciated that.

To my dear friends Ed and Brad who provided support during the process. Your friendship gave me the incentive to retire in San Diego.

To Jimmy V, Brian, Blair, and Brent whose work on behalf of our largest client was second to none. But of more value was the friendship and trips that allowed me to have a sense of tradition at a time when work was my top priority.

To Christopher, who made us think of our book as more than a business book. Your effort to develop these "instincts" provides us with an amazing sense of pride and inspiration.

And, finally, to those who worked along side me at Barkley Evergreen and Partners and allowed me to serve as your president and CEO. You were my extended family and circle of friends. You provided me the most glorious of times and for that I thank you from the bottom of my heart.

From Pattye

To Mom and Dad: I am who I am today because of your love, care, and wisdom. Thank you for teaching me to have a positive attitude and to believe in myself. And, most of all, thank you for helping raise my girls and for always being there.

To my family: Mark, you are the most generous, caring, loving, and supportive husband of all time. Thank you for putting up with all the long hours and for always being there for me. It's my turn to be there for you.

To my beautiful daughters: Melissa (who told me she doesn't need to read the book because she saw the movie!), thank you for playing such a starring role in my life. I have cherished every moment (and there have been too few) we've had together and I am so looking forward to the rest of our journey. You are smart and caring and have become a lovely young woman with a bright future.

Lindsey: What an incredible treat it is for me to be around and watch you grow into a compassionate and wonderful young lady. You keep me laughing and, yes, you have to read the book! I'm looking forward to being there for your exciting journey.

To Dave Gillogly: You took an impressionable college intern in her first real job and showed her that leaders can lead with Christian values. I learned so much from you about leading with integrity and compassion and about giving back.

To Steve Lynn and Bob Flack: Thank you for seeing something in me that I didn't know was there and for taking a chance on me.

To Ron Beasley: You are the world's greatest executive coach. I don't know where I would be without your insight.

To Rena Rhoades: You managed my life and touched my heart. Thanks for keeping me on course all those years.

And, finally, to all the incredible colleagues, friends, and partners I worked with over the years at Sonic: You are the best and the brightest people I have ever worked with. Thank you for allowing me to help you build the Sonic brand. What a grand time we had.

Introduction

What Exactly Is a Corner Office Instinct?

An *instinct* is a gut feeling, an intuition, or even a sixth sense. Your instincts guide your behavior. In many cases, they are often a survival tool and they kick in when you need them.

That's why we talk about survival instincts, basic instincts, natural instincts, and even killer instincts. No one talks about business instincts, though, particularly the kind that can land you in the corner office. That's why we call them *Corner Office Instincts.* These instincts don't just automatically kick in when you need them. They need to be identified, nurtured, developed, and practiced on a *daily basis.*

Let's face it. Being successful in business is about mastering the arts of survival and behavior. Every day at work, you will be judged by your instantaneous reactions to circumstances. If you react in an inappropriate, insincere, or insensitive manner at the wrong time in front of the wrong people—well, buckle up because the ride is about to get bumpy. More careers are lost by the inability to master the soft skills of leadership—the ones guided by your instincts.

Don't let the term *soft skills* mislead you into dismissing their importance.

How you build and maintain relationships, motivate those around you, instill confidence in all who work with you, and maintain an impressive level of self-awareness can make or break your career. Based on our own successes, mistakes, and our observations of many great leaders, we have identified seven Attitude Instincts, which speak to the mental preparation side of business, and eight Performance Instincts, which speak to your actions and work product.

Both Attitude and Performance Instincts are critical for the journey to the corner office. We talk a lot about getting to the corner office, but that is really just a term for achieving success. Getting to the corner office can mean literally getting wherever *you* want to be, being successful at building your department or organization, owning your own business, being a top volunteer for a nonprofit organization, or successfully running your household as CEO. The corner office is whatever and wherever you want it to be to satisfy your definition of success. These Corner Office Instincts work in all these circumstances and more.

Each chapter highlights an instinct and provides a guide to help you understand why that particular instinct is important.

To succeed, you must be aware of these instincts, and you must find ways to practice them and identify when they are in use. We believe our examples, stories, and questions will help you use your instincts as a guide to *your* corner office.

I | Attitude Instincts

1 Get Married Again—Your Spouse Won't Mind

Pattye: Our readers may find this hard to believe, but I would have never made it to the corner office without your help.

Scott: Now, why would our readers find it so hard to believe that you needed my help?

Pattye: Actually, I think most people don't want to admit that they can't do something on their own. But I know for a fact that I couldn't have done it without you there to push me, to encourage me, to make me look smarter, to give me confidence when I was shaking in my boots—the list could go on and on.

Scott: I'm all ears because this is good for my ego.

Pattye: Oh, I'm not sure your ego is in any need of repair.

Scott: Point taken, and here is a little secret for you, Ms. Moore. The fact is I couldn't have gotten to the top without your help either. I can't even count how many times I bounced ideas off you, tested out personnel decisions, and asked your opinion.

Pattye: If this was a self-help book, you might say we were codependent—in a good way.

Scott: But since it's a book about leadership, I have a better term—Corporate Soul Mates. That is truly what we were for 12 years, and what we still are. It is a unique concept and probably the secret to our success. It is sort of like being married without the expense of anniversary gifts.

What is a friend? A single soul in two bodies.

—Aristotle

What is a Corporate Soul Mate? A single soul in two bodies.

—Scott and Pattye

Corner Office Instinct 1

Find a Corporate Soul Mate

Soul mate (n.): partner, colleague, supporter, ally, helper, confidante

In a recent Monster.com survey, employees were asked which Olympic sport their typical workday most resembled. Fifty-two percent of the respondents said "the luge"—in other words, they feel like they are racing 80 mph on their own. Only 20 percent of respondents said "bobsled"—which requires teamwork *to win the race.*

The luge is a pretty apt description for life in corporate America—hurtling through the day at breakneck speeds, basically one sharp turn away from losing control. And, knowing (or believing, at least) that it's all up to you. You've certainly heard the adage that it's lonely at the top, but for most workers, it's lonely on the way there as well. And most people believe that this is just the way it is—a dog-eat-dog world and you are on your own.

It doesn't have to be that way. In fact, if you really want to be the best, it *can't* be that way. And we are living proof of that.

Our success can be attributed in large part to our ability to embrace, practice, and live one of the most overlooked corner office instincts. Our instinct told us that we had a unique working relationship, but it told us something more. Our instinct told us it was okay to break the paradigm of an arm's-length agency/client relationship and, as a result, we became corporate confidantes. Our instinct pushed us to evolve from confidantes to corporate soul mates—two leaders who depended on and needed each other to challenge and debate the business issues of the day. When we did this, we discovered that it brought out the best and brightest thinking in each other. And that, my friends, is the power and benefit of having a corporate soul mate.

In order for the corporate soul mate instinct to pay dividends, however, there must be a foundation of unconditional trust and honesty between the two of you. *Honesty* in the sense that your relationship is so secure that neither of you holds anything back nor has any fear of being judged. *Trust* in the sense that regardless of what or who you talk about, what is said between the two of you remains confidential. It is only in a low-risk, nonjudgmental, confidential environment that you can truly be soul mates.

The reality is that there are situations at work almost every day where you need a corporate soul mate. Whether you own your business, are working your way up, or are already there, you will encounter new challenges, and you will be asked to step out of your comfort zone. You will often be uncertain as to what is the right decision.

You can internalize this uncertainty, talk to your spouse (who, by the way, might be a perfect corporate soul mate—don't automatically exclude him or her), ask your dog for advice, or you can consciously seek out someone to be your ally, confidante, supporter, friend, and corporate soul mate.

Who's Your Spotter?

Another way to think about this is to consider how helpful it is to have a workout partner at the gym. With a workout partner, you have someone to hold you accountable, to help you stay motivated, to encourage you, and to help you get back on track when you slack off. Most important, that workout partner gives you the confidence to stretch beyond what is comfortable, and, as a result, you reach new heights and keep improving your personal bests. Getting to the corner office is quite a workout, and you need encouragement, motivation, and help every bit as much as you do in the gym.

This instinct is one that came very naturally to both of us. For the past 12 years, we've been each other's corporate soul mate and have pushed each other to new career heights.

Joined at the Hip

My relationship with Scott started as the typical client/agency relationship. It was clear that he was very smart and knew the restaurant business so I was glad to have him working on our account. It wasn't long, however, before we both realized that we had a unique opportunity to form an even stronger bond that would pay dividends for both of us and our companies. The passion we each had for the business and for solving problems was evident in the late-night phone calls to report what we had just seen at a competitor or to share an idea that was sparked by something on television. Our curiosity and desire to be the best led us to bounce ideas off each other for growing our own businesses, for solving tough personnel issues, or for our own development. Pretty soon, our "souls" had become so connected that you might mistake us for a married couple (hence the title of this chapter—Get Married

Again). We were truly joined at the hip, and, truth be told, still are. We still consult with each other several times a day.

—Pattye

The Rest of the Story

Although Pattye described our partnership well, I don't think you will really "get it" unless I give you more specifics about what it meant for us to be corporate soul mates. Here are a few examples:

- Most nights we touched base (after Pattye got her children to bed) to talk about burning issues, upcoming meetings or presentations, or simply to compare notes after visiting competitors for dinner.
- We still laugh about a 6:30 A.M. phone call getting ready for a big presentation one day. I was at the office trying to fax a final presentation to her at home but both our fax machines were out of paper. We spent 30 minutes trying to help each other load fax paper—unsuccessfully, I might add.
- I remember helping her work through tough Arthritis Foundation decisions when she was chair. And I remember her listening to me work through tough personnel decisions.
- I read drafts of her speeches while she read drafts of mine. We rehearsed in front of each other because no one else was as brutally honest.
- I had to sit by her on airplanes (see Chapter 9).

- She will tell you she became president of Sonic because I made her smarter and better. I will tell you I became chairman and CEO of Barkley Evergreen & Partners because she made me smarter and better.
- I cried when she left Sonic because half of me left as well. She cried (with joy) when I left the agency because it meant we would be working together again.
- We get mad, we fuss, we yell and scream at each other, and we make each other's brains hurt. But we know what each other is capable of and we won't settle for less.

This, ladies and gentlemen, is what it means to be corporate soul mates. What are you waiting for?

—Scott

Note to spouses and significant others: This concept of corporate soul mates may test the strength of your relationship. It may seem to you that your partner has found "someone else." If you are the suspicious type, your mind could easily wander and you could begin to doubt your partner's motivation. There will be late-night and weekend phone calls, e-mails that go back and forth so quickly they might as well be in a chat room. And there will be meetings and trips together. It would be easy to get jealous or suspicious, but if it's a true corporate soul mate, you have nothing to worry about. Listen in—at least until you nod off because all you will hear is obsessive conversations about work. Besides, think of all the times you don't have to pretend to be listening and sympathetic to the issue du jour or pending crisis!

The idea of having a partner shouldn't come as a big surprise because many of the great accomplishments in any field have come from two people working together; for example:

- Lewis and Clark
- Columbus and Queen Isabella
- Madame Curie and Louis Pasteur
- Hanna/Barbera
- Ben and Jerry
- Hewlett/Packard
- Bill Gates and Paul Allen
- Larry Page and Sergey Brin

Heck, even the Lone Ranger had a corporate soul mate—Tonto.

In every one of these cases, it's easy to envision the conversations, the late night arguments, the debates, and the decisions to go for it, to try something new.

And, just like jumping off the high diving board as a child for the first time, the jump and flight into new territory didn't seem quite so risky when we were holding our best friend's hand on the way down. Therein lies the ultimate benefit of a corporate soul mate.

A corporate soul mate provides that hand to squeeze as you jump, and from that squeeze comes the confidence and self-assuredness needed to lead others. This confidence is critical because it often determines how passionate others will become about your vision. And the level of passion in those you lead often determines your success as a leader.

Why Do You Not Have a Corporate Soul Mate?

We are willing to wager that most of you reading this book don't have a corporate soul mate. As we talked to colleagues and business associates around the country, we discovered that most people don't have anyone to confide in, to encourage them, or to challenge them.

Warning: We must warn you that just finding someone you can confide in does not a corporate soul mate make. Going to lunch with the same peer and venting about all your problems at work may be therapeutic for you, but it is not the relationship we are describing. You are not seeking counsel, you are not asking for a critique of your performance, or help on which direction to take—you are venting. A corporate soul mate goes a bit deeper than venting.

If you don't have a corporate soul mate, don't be alarmed because you are not alone. You might want to think about the reasons why you don't. Do any of the following hit home?

Here from the home office of INSTINCTS LLC are the top 10 reasons for not having a corporate soul mate:

10. You don't trust anyone as it relates to your career, except yourself. *You alone are out to disprove the theory that no man is an island—good luck.*
9. Your boyfriend says he doesn't like you spending so much time with the new marketing director of your client. *Maybe you two should work on those trust issues.*
8. You resent sharing the spotlight. *With an ego like that, good luck finding someone to be your corporate soul mate.*
7. You can't rely on a female as a corporate soul mate—what would the guys say? *You've got bigger issues than we can focus on.*
6. You tried it once but it just didn't work. *So you think giving up easily will get you to the corner office?*

5. You'd like one but you're not quite sure how to find one or how to use one. *Keep reading!*
4. You don't want anyone telling you what to do and, more important, you don't want anyone to know you don't have all the answers—they could use that against you. *Get therapy!*
3. You don't have the time. *We guess you don't have the drive to make it to the corner office either.*
2. You prefer a venting partner because it is more fun to be a fire starter rather than a firefighter. *Your own career is likely to go up in flames.*
1. You don't understand the need to have one. After all, no one is as smart as you. *We look forward to reading your new book.*

Corporate Soul Mates Are Not Your College Drinking Buddies

Let us repeat that. Corporate soul mates are not your college drinking buddies or your best friend from high school. It's great to have friends, but the chances are they don't work in your company or your industry, and they are not going to understand your particular challenges or issues. A true corporate soul mate should be someone:

- You respect, admire, and trust, and who is at a similar level or position.
- You think is smarter than you, but who is equally passionate about what he or she does.
- Who works either at your company, for a vendor, in your industry, or in a related field.
- You work with on community/civic boards. We've found some of our best corporate soul mates this way.

Once you've found that person or persons (by the way, there is no rule that you can only have one), invite them to lunch and ask them for advice. If it's a good fit, you will naturally start to seek each other out more and more. If it's not a good fit, move on.

Pay particular attention to those who work at competitive firms. Seek out and build relationships with competitors you respect and admire. Make a point as the years roll by to stay in touch with them. Even though they may not have been a candidate at that time for a corporate soul mate, jobs and careers change.

From Most Feared Competitor to Most Valued Corporate Soul Mate

For years, Tom Millweard ran the Pizza Hut account for his agency in Dallas and I ran it for my agency in Houston. We each tried to secure more and more business, most likely at the expense of the other. As much as I wanted to beat him every time, I have to admit I had a great amount of respect for how Tom ran his business and how he serviced the client. Years later, as president of an agency in Kansas City, I found myself in need of a corporate soul mate internally. I needed to find someone who wasn't afraid to tell me when I had a bad idea and someone with whom I could have unconditional trust as to how he handled issues with clients and personnel.

I flew down to Dallas and asked Tom, my greatest competitor over the years, to come help me grow this agency. He did. We joined forces and I could not have asked for a more honest, trustworthy confidante and advisor. He was not afraid to tell me when he thought I was wrong, and I always appreciated that he felt he could say what was on his mind without fear of some adolescent response on my part. We grew the agency to record highs, but most important, we had a glorious time doing it.

—*Scott*

Conclusion

There is something we want you to be mindful of as you progress in your career. Over the years, we all pick up subtle and not so subtle signals that shape our behavior subconsciously. Some of these signals are good and others are bad. One bad signal we all get is that *reaching out* can often be seen as a sign of weakness. We strongly advise *against* taking this to heart. Our 12 years together of pushing, trusting, challenging, laughing, and crying has allowed us to move forward in each of our careers with a higher level of confidence that our decisions were the right ones for the time. We didn't have to take our partnership to the extreme—but we did. The choice is yours.

Just remember, like the story we told you, half the fun is the journey. We absolutely guarantee that it won't be as much fun or as rewarding if you go it alone.

Five Questions to Ask Yourself to See if You Have the Instinct to Find a Corporate Soul Mate

1. Do you have a late night or weekend conversation with the same person about work on a very frequent basis?
2. Is there one person you immediately call when you have a new idea or see something intriguing that might work for your business?

3. When you've got a tough decision to make, do you immediately reach out for help from this one person first?
4. Do your kids think that (fill in the blank) is a relative?
5. Is there someone who understands how you think?

If you answered yes to all of these questions, then you indeed have a corporate soul mate. Here's a more difficult question: Would that person answer yes to these questions about you? We hope so.

Five Steps You Can Take to Begin Developing the Instinct to Find a Corporate Soul Mate

1. Make a list of people with whom you work closely and/or with whom you are friends. Then write down times you've gone to them for help and gauge how helpful it was. Be honest.
2. Examine your list—does anyone stand out as consistently being your "go to" person? If so, you might have a soul mate.
3. If not, make another list. This time, go beyond the usual suspects—the names you came up with quickly. What about someone at church or on the community or charity board with you? Someone you talk to at the fitness center?
4. Once you've identified some potential folks, go for a trial run. Invite them to lunch. Call and ask for advice. (People love this, by the way—wouldn't you?)
5. Feed and water regularly. Marriages need care. Friendships need attention. And corporate soul mates disappear if not fed and watered regularly.

2 What's Love Got to Do with It?

Scott: I can't think of anyone I know who works as hard as you.

Pattye: That's crazy. We all work hard, don't we?

Scott: Oh come on, Wal-Mart was closed more than you! Even when we finished that marathon day of meetings in Houston, you announced we were renting a car instead of flying home.

Pattye: Hey now, that was a good idea and you know it.

Scott: Not many would call spending eight hours hitting every Sonic Drive-In and all the other fast-food competitors from Houston to Oklahoma City a good idea. But, no, you were on a quest for new ideas—or maybe you were just hungry.

Pattye: I can't help it if you never learned to pace yourself. How many times did I tell you—just take one bite and throw the rest away?

Scott: If I hadn't hijacked the keys, we'd have ended up in an emergency room. I have to say, though, you were unbelievably passionate about the Sonic business.

Pattye: You were quite the trouper for enduring an eight-hour discussion and shopping the competition.

Scott: Was that a discussion? I only remember cheeseburgers, fries, shakes, and antacid medicine.

Choose a job you love, and you will never have to work a day in your life.

—Confucius

If you don't love what you do, you can't lead from the heart.

—Scott and Pattye

Corner Office Instinct 2

Have a Passionate Love Affair with the Office

Love (n.): being devoted to, being keen on, finding irresistible

According to a recent survey from the Conference Board, less than half of all Americans are satisfied with their jobs—the highest level of discontent since the survey was first conducted in 1995. The decline in job satisfaction is found among workers of all ages across all income brackets and regions.

We have good news and bad news for you. We'll start with the bad news. We're going to talk about how important it is to *love* your job and, apparently, less than half of you even *like* it. There's a big gap between love and like.

The good news is that with less than half of all Americans even liking their jobs, the pool of competition for the corner office just got smaller. How do you take advantage of a smaller pool? We have one word for you: passion.

When you are passionate about your profession and you have an *insatiable* and *irresistible* interest in all it entails, you have taken the first step toward the corner office. This professional submersion will allow you to convert ambitions into accomplishments.

Many may think it quite unusual to link love to the workplace (unless you are speaking of a sordid romance). We have found the love affair between workers and their careers to be one of the most important requirements for getting to the corner office.

Note to the ambitious: Don't take this to mean that you only need to love your job—it goes much deeper. You must also love and have an unwavering pride in the company, the people you work with, and, perhaps most important, the industry you work in.

It Was Ad Agency or Bust!

Before I ever landed my first job in the ad agency business, I knew it was what I wanted and where I would spend my life. From my freshman class in Advertising 101 (which caused me to switch majors), I wanted to get into that industry and I wanted it badly. If you're lucky like me, you'll discover early something that intrigues you. For me, it was advertising. I loved the fact that I would be selling ideas. So I loaded up the unair-conditioned Pinto and headed for Houston, where a friend lived. I landed a job making $30,000 (an amazing starting salary in 1979) as a project coordinator for a homebuilder. At the end of the first day, I left my hard hat in the trailer with a note that said I quit. I quit because my heart knew it wasn't the advertising agency business.

I went on to work at a jewelry in-house print department, but I hated it for the same reason—it wasn't the advertising agency business. I switched gears and waited tables at an all-night diner where at 3:00 A.M. there was no telling what characters I would be waiting on. I did this so that I could wait "it" out—my opportunity. I was sleeping on the floor at a friend's apartment, praying I was going to get something, anything, at a real ad agency. I was finally offered an entry-level job managing the Ronald McDonald program at Winius Brandon advertising agency. They paid me a starting salary of $900 a month. Art Casper and Bill Blumberg gave me a shot, and because of them, I have never looked back and have never felt richer.

—*Scott*

Are You in Love with Your Profession?

Your job, your company, and the industry—these are the three worlds that make up your professional life. Too many people ignore the last two. They only look at the perks and the title and become mercenaries for hire with a single goal: to get to that corner office. If they don't love all three worlds, you can imagine the rape and plundering that will go on.

To find out if the corner office is potentially in your future, administer a brutally honest self-assessment of desire, dedication, and determination. Be aware of your head and be true to your heart when asking yourself: Do you genuinely love, and are you driven by *what* you do, *the company* you work for, and the *industry* in which it competes?

Pity the executive who leaves an occupation he loves to take a job with a bigger salary and loftier title in an industry he has no passion for or the unfortunate radio executive who, though he dreamed of and loves the industry, sells a format that he finds so boring he can't even bring himself to program it on his car radio. They may have good jobs with great salaries, but the reality is neither will ever land in the corner office.

Too Many Love Affairs to Count

As I reflect back on my career, I realize I've had a lot of love affairs—with my work. I can honestly say I've loved every job I've had, starting with my first job as a teenager. I've worked in retail, in government, for a major energy company, for an advertising agency, for a fast-food chain, and now for myself. I've done everything from cashier to secretary to marketing to senior management. How can I say I've loved all those different jobs, industries, and people? There's certainly not a common denominator among them—except my attitude and outlook.

My parents taught me several valuable lessons that have shaped my approach to work and life. They taught and showed me that happiness doesn't come from what happens to you; it comes from what you do with what you have. It's all up to me to either make the best or the worst of any given situation. Because of those lessons, I don't recall spending time thinking about whether I was happy or not in a given job. I just remember figuring out what I needed to do to make the best of something, and that almost always involved getting to know the people, the company, and the industry. Once I did that, it was easy to fall in love and be happy.

—*Pattye*

When you create a world in which you genuinely love your job, company, and industry, you will find a welcome addition to your passion—curiosity. As long as you remain curious, you will undoubtedly grow, both professionally and personally, at a rate far faster than your peers.

Curiosity is not only a by-product of loving your work and all it entails; it also serves as a catalyst by providing you the needed adrenaline and drive to obtain additional knowledge and insight. This knowledge and insight is what will set you apart.

Who Do You Bet on to Reach the Corner Office First?

Perhaps you are in a situation where you love just one, or two, of the three worlds in your professional life. Our question then is, "How curious are you?"

You would be surprised how many people say they don't like their jobs, yet in the same breath, they expect to be promoted. These are the same people who can't tell you the pressing issues for their company or the hurdles their clients are facing. The reason they can't tell you is because they use their job description as a rationale for a lack of curiosity. Have you ever heard, "That's not my job"? Those with the instinct to make it to the corner office use their job description as a passport and a license to learn anything and everything.

Love Is Curious

Some people might have called it obsession, but to me, it was truly love. I loved the Sonic brand, the Sonic franchisees and operators, and the crazy, unpredictable fast-food industry. It wasn't love at first sight, but it was a love and passion that grew as I got to know the people and learned the business. There was nothing I liked better than spending time at our drive-ins and listening to the operators, managers, and crewmembers talk about their successes, challenges, and ideas. I also loved listening to customers. Curiosity helped fan my passion because I was insanely interested in what was working, what wasn't, and why some drive-ins performed better than others. That curiosity allowed me to know wonderful people, and it paved the way to great ideas, and created an incredible love affair with work for me. I realize now that you can't have love without curiosity.

—Pattye

There is no shortcut to the corner office (unless Dad owns the company). To those who want to bypass the journey of commitment and sacrifice to simply get there, we offer a word of advice: Save your time. Without creating a love affair with your career, odds are you will only get into a corner office by appointment.

This instinct is listed second because we believe it to be one of the most crucial. Love and passion for your professional life, and the ambition that goes with it, serve as a platform for you to develop and refine the remaining instincts.

Conclusion

In response to the chapter title "What's Love Got to Do with It?" our answer is, "Everything." Those who are the best love what they do, and they love it for the right reasons. It's time to ask yourself, "Do you?"

Five Questions to Ask Yourself to See if You Have the Instinct of Being in Love with the Office

1. Do you refer to it as a career versus a job?
2. Would you ever move to another city to advance your career?
3. Do you read business books in your spare time instead of novels?

4. Are you obsessed by the thought of breaking some new ground at your company?
5. Do you listen to those above you intently and take in both the good and the bad?

If you answered yes to all these questions, congratulations! You're in love with the office and on your way up. If not, give yourself a chance to fall in love by taking the following actions.

Five Steps to Develop the Instinct of Being in Love with the Office

1. Look at how you answered the previous questions. If you answered "no" to two or more questions, chances are you don't love what you do and it's time to reengineer your career path.
2. Do some soul searching. If you do not love what you do, is it because you are in the wrong job, the wrong company, or because you lack curiosity?
3. If you are in the wrong place, don't be afraid to make a needed change.
4. Don't assume you can't get excited about your work. True, many people don't, but they aren't reading this book, are they?
5. Get involved in your company outside of your specific job description. Join a committee, a task force, an employee group—anything that will allow you to see your company from a new and different perspective. Then, extend yourself beyond your workplace by getting involved in industry trade associations. Finally, spend time imagining in detail where you want to take your career. Get excited about the destination and draw yourself a road map of how to get there. Don't forget that you need to be just as excited about the journey as the destination.

3 Put Down Your Fingers and Listen

Pattye: You know what really bugs me?

Scott: Besides me not answering my phone? No, what?

Pattye: People sending BlackBerry messages when I'm making a presentation. It's really disheartening to look at your audience only to discover that half of them are staring down into their laps and *blacking*—that's a new word created just for this action, believe it or not.

Scott: Okay, how do I say this? Maybe your presentations need work.

Pattye: Very funny. Companies spend money to bring in speakers or to send people to meetings, and all the participants do is check their e-mails.

Scott: Hold on there, I agree this is becoming a big problem, but don't be so sure they are checking their e-mails. And, well, before we go any farther, I have a confession to make.

Pattye: So, you're going to tell me you check and send messages while I'm talking?

Scott: I will neither confirm nor deny the accusation, your honor.

Pattye: Spill it.

Scott: Well, since you put it that way—technically, I don't have to tell you since you said it first! But, yes, a work associate and I may have sent some messages to each other in meetings. It's possible one of those could have been sent—not saying it was—when you were presenting.

Pattye: So, you weren't checking e-mails, you were talking to each other while I was presenting?

Scott: But, we were quiet, weren't we?

Pattye: Let me guess—you also have a habit of checking e-mail while you're on the phone with someone.

Scott: I thought that's what multitasking meant.

Pattye: Well, I have to confess, I'm guilty of all of the above, but I am in a recovery program. I do have one *very* important tip for our readers: *Do not send your boss an e-mail, or reply to an e-mail from him, while you are on a conference call with him.* This is experience talking.

Scott: Ouch.

No man ever listened himself out of a job.

—Calvin Coolidge

Lots of people have "talked" themselves out of jobs.

—Scott and Pattye

Corner Office Instinct 3

If Someone Is Talking to You, Return the Favor and Listen

Listen (v.): make a conscious effort to hear, to pay attention

A recent study by an executive recruitment firm, Korn/Ferry International, discovered that 80 percent of business executives worldwide are constantly connected to work through a laptop, a cell phone, a PDA, or another mobile device.

You may ask, however, if a whole chapter on listening is really necessary. Well, based on our 50+ combined years of experience, it's more than necessary. It's absolutely essential. We believe that corporate executives are losing their ability to truly listen. In fact, we think this deterioration is reaching epidemic proportions.

Time and time again, we have sat in meetings and witnessed senior executives pulling out their BlackBerries and reading and responding to e-mails. All of this happens while someone else is talking. Our fear is that reading and responding to e-mails during meetings has become so commonplace that executives no longer even regard their behavior as being rude, disrespectful, or insulting. Not only have executives stopped considering it rude, we believe subordinates see this behavior as acceptable and copy it. *It is not acceptable.* It is no different than pulling out a magazine in the middle of a meeting and reading it. This, ladies and gentlemen, is an epidemic of disrespect, and what concerns us is that those spreading it don't view it as wrong. Instead, they see it as a badge of efficiency.

It is virtually impossible to attend a meeting where PDAs and cell phones are not present, and it is even rarer to find them turned off. Here is a novel thought. Instead of being consumed by instant communications with the office, why not have instant and ongoing engagement with those in your meeting? Listen to them—you might be amazed at what you hear.

We would love to see every business meeting start with the same announcement: "Will everyone please turn off your BlackBerries, Treos, and cell phones and place them in the basket on the back table. You can reclaim them at the completion of the meeting—now, on to the agenda."

If you want to be an effective leader, listening is an art that you will need to learn and master. If you want a fast track to the corner office, then listen up (pun intended), because great listening skills will help you get there quickly.

As with many of the other instincts, there is good news—if you're willing to listen. If you master the art of listening and practice it diligently, you will stand out in the crowd. Trust us when we say you will not have much competition because no one takes the time to truly listen anymore—particularly in corporate America. It is a phenomenon that we have both witnessed firsthand (and have been guilty of), and it amazes and disgusts us.

What Did You Say?

> I'm sorry, but I was so busy thinking about what I was going to say to IMPRESS people that I actually didn't hear what you said. Was it important? Could you repeat just the parts that are

important to me and that will help me get ahead? Actually, on second thought, could you just send me an e-mail about it? That way I can read it when I'm supposed to be listening to someone else.

The above comments seem ridiculous, but if we're being honest here, it's exactly what is going on in business today. People are so caught up in what is unnecessary instant communication via the newest technology that they forget to, or choose not to, listen.

We believe people don't stop listening until they become adults and, most specifically, until they start to succeed in business. As with many of the other instincts, this one gets passed over on your way up the ladder. Almost everyone now has instant access to their e-mails, so there is constant competition for the attention of corporate America. Do I listen to the speaker, or do I click and scroll with every new vibration that signals an unread piece of communication? We are sorry to say the winner is too often the BlackBerry, and the executive mentally departs the meeting to scroll down and read. When this occurs, listening has stopped.

There's another irony at work here. Many people accept the concept that you need to ask questions and be curious if you want to get ahead. But that is only half of the solution. What gets forgotten is that you need to actually listen to the answers. Too many times, we have seen executives ask questions and then get distracted with their e-mails while someone is earnestly trying to answer them.

Hello? Is Anyone There?

I was very fortunate to have an incredible listener as my boss at my first job out of college. He was such a good listener, though, that it was pretty unnerving at first. I'd rush into his office to talk about a problem or an issue and would just blurt out what was going on—probably without taking a breath. I'd stop to wait for his response. But he usually said nothing. He would just look at me and wait. When this first happened, I remember thinking, "Maybe he's deaf" or "Maybe I just thought all those things, but actually haven't said them out loud yet." Of course, I rushed in to fill the silence—sometimes with more ramblings, but occasionally with good thoughts, and, maybe even a solution or two. When I asked him why he was always so quiet, he said that he learned much more by listening to me than by talking and that good listening required patience to make sure the person talking was finished. Wow! What a concept, and a great early lesson. I wish I had applied it more consistently.

—Pattye

If You Listen Carefully, You'll Hear an Idea Being Born

"No Talking" Signs Don't Belong Only in the Library

Can anyone remember ever seeing a "No Talking" sign anywhere, except in libraries? Those famous signs were a symbol for thinking, reading, and learning. We don't believe we've seen them anywhere else, and we're not sure if they are even present in libraries anymore. What a shame. We think they should be posted periodically throughout all retail establishments and business offices as well.

Why retail establishments? Let us ask you how many times you have been behind people in line who can't stop talking long enough on their cell phones to give an order. They slow the process down and often get something wrong because they don't have the common courtesy to cut short their conversations. Must we all be exposed to people's conversations when all we want to do is order some food? The answer is no. But once again, it does not enter the consciousness that this behavior is rude to the employee and to those waiting in line.

My Heroes: Big City Bagels in San Diego

I can't tell you how happy I was the other day when I walked into my favorite bagel shop Big City Bagels in San Diego. There on the counter was a sign that read, "We will not take your order if you are on the phone." Hooray. Someone has finally sent the message that if we can't have your attention, you will not receive our attention. I applaud the owners, and I only hope some of the national chains begin to follow this lead.

—Scott

When we *listen,* something amazing happens. The cycle of idea generation begins to simmer. The beauty of a big idea is that the stimulus can come from anyone or anything. Play along with us for a moment.

Imagine there are 20 executives in the audience, and a presentation is made. There are no questions at the conclusion; however, at any given time, half of the executives checked and responded to a minimum of two e-mails on their BlackBerries.

Now, that same presentation occurs, but all BlackBerries and cell phones are put away. At the end of the presentation, there are several questions based on what the executives *heard.* From those questions, comes a discussion that leads to an idea for a new product line or a new process that saves the company money.

We admit the example is elementary, but if you don't hear it, you can't build on it. Big ideas are built—they don't just show up.

We are *all* guilty of not listening—your authors included. Instead of listening, observing, and learning, we're reading, responding, and looking away—all done very discreetly, of course, as if that matters.

But we now get to assume the role of reformed smokers who tell everyone they come into contact with how much the smokers need to quit. Just in case you think we are being too reactionary in this caution, consider the following. A work associate told us recently that there is now a name for dropping your BlackBerry in your lap, tuning out the meeting, and starting to type or scroll. It is called the "BlackBerry prayer position." The *Wall Street Journal* on December 8, 2006, ran an article entitled "BlackBerry Orphans," talking about the negative impact of the use of a BlackBerry on children and families. Apparently, we are not the only ones who feel this is reaching epidemic proportions.

It would do everyone some good to go back to the lesson we were all taught in kindergarten: "You don't talk when someone else is talking." You may ask if it is the same as talking if you are typing or reading, and the answer is *yes.*

If you don't take time to listen and to think, how will you innovate? If you don't listen to your customers, your colleagues, your peers, and your competitors, where will you get your inspiration? It is truly amazing how many ideas could be sparked if you just listen to people.

Listen to Your Frontline Employees—You'll Be Amazed

As I mentioned earlier, one of my favorite things to do was visiting Sonic Drive-Ins and talking to crewmembers. Yes, I liked the food and all the exciting travel, but what I really liked most was listening to our crewmembers. They had the most amazing ideas and insights on the business. By asking them the right questions and then actually listening to their answers, we were able to make many changes, modifications, and additions to a variety of things, from uniforms to training to new products. The crewmembers were the source of most of "my" ideas and innovations. Gaining all that knowledge only took two ears.

—*Pattye*

Can You Learn How to Listen?

It's easy to learn how to listen. It's fun. It's quick and it's portable—you can take it anywhere with you. Just follow these six easy steps. It only takes 16 hours of practice each day. It's so simple, even an adult can learn to do this.

While we're having some tongue-in-cheek fun with this, we're serious about the fact that you can "relearn" how to listen. It does, however, require practice every waking hour and constant attention to and awareness of what you're doing. It can be easier, however, than a weight-loss program, an exercise regime, or learning German in three weeks.

Based on what we've learned by listening very intently to a number of very wise leaders over the years, we've outlined some thoughts and ideas that may help you hone those listening skills and tune up those out-of-shape, underperforming ears of yours. Here are a few suggestions:

- Listen actively. We learned this term from one of our favorite consultants—Connie Williams with Synectics. She introduced the phrase "active listening" to us. It makes sense. The best way to ensure that you're truly listening to someone is to take part in the conversation. Ask questions that clarify or build on an idea. You'll be less likely to do other things if you are fully engaged. *Note to parents:* Active listening is really important with your kids. They will call you on it every time you don't do this.
- Create specific listening sessions with employees, customers, and peers. We borrowed this idea from Chet Cadieux at QuikTrip Corporation. Once a year, he has an item on his board meeting agenda called "Listening Session." It's time set aside so he can do nothing but listen to board member ideas, thoughts, and concerns.
- Spend time out in the field for your profession or civic organization. Make it a point to walk around and just observe and listen. Don't have an agenda, and don't pontificate. Just listen. Maybe ask a few questions, but don't comment.
- Hold staff meetings with the sole purpose of asking people what they're hearing out there. If you haven't been doing this, it will be quite puzzling at first when people walk into a meeting and you simply ask, "So, what are you hearing

out there?" Ask the question and then shut up. Not only will *you* eventually learn some interesting things, but you'll also mentor and teach your staff.

- Celebrate ideas, innovations, and changes that come as a direct result of something someone heard—out in the field, from employees and customers, and so on. Make a big deal of this.

PATTYE: I always wanted to encourage operators to call me with product ideas. During my speech at the Sonic conventions, I made a point of acknowledging and thanking an operator by name who suggested a new idea. It didn't matter whether we actually took the idea to market it not. The point was to let people know that my ears were open for business and that I actually heard what they were saying.

- Recognize and repeat after us: "I will always be smarter if I don't try to have all the ideas or solutions myself. The only way I can get ideas from others is to take time to hear what they have to say."

Conclusion

Listening is good for business. It's definitely good for your career, your marriage, and your relationships with your friends and your children. Great listeners are usually described as empathetic, in-tune, personable, and caring. Think about the teachers, bosses, mentors, and friends who have made the biggest impact in your life. Odds are good that they were all great listeners. Join their club and you *will* make a difference as a leader.

Five Questions to Ask Yourself to See if You Have the Instinct of Listening

1. Have you ever checked e-mail or sent messages during a presentation?
2. Do you try to multitask by continuing to read e-mails or type messages while on the phone or talking to someone in your office?
3. Can you repeat a person's name shortly after being introduced?
4. Has a friend or spouse ever accused you of not listening?
5. Do you have a habit of interrupting people when they are talking so you can talk?

If you answered no, no, yes, no, and no, then you have highly developed listening skills. If not, stop checking your e-mail and read on.

Five Steps to Develop the Instinct of Listening

1. Make a vow to never check messages when sitting in a meeting or at a presentation. If you must respond, leave the room.
2. If someone comes into your office to talk to you, *take your hands off the keyboard* and give them your full attention. If it's a bad time, tell them so and reschedule.
3. At least once a day, ask someone their opinion and listen to their answer.
4. Ask your spouse or children to tell you something interesting that happened today. Don't ask, "How was your day?" The perfunctory "Fine" doesn't require you to listen actively.
5. Prearrange a secret signal from a trusted colleague (corporate soul mate) to let you know if you are talking too much or interrupting others—in other words, not listening.

4 Of Course I Want Your Opinion—As Long as It Is the Same as Mine

Scott: Do you know the one thing I valued most about our agency/client relationship?

Pattye: Okay, I know a trick question when I hear one. Let me guess, the spacious Oklahoma City airport?

Scott: Hmm, hadn't thought of that, even though Floyd, the security guard, and I were on a first-name basis.

Pattye: Well, that's special—do the two of you exchange holiday cards as well? Let's see, was it all the free burgers you got at our taste testings?

Scott: Damn, another good one. I have to tell you, for a single guy, that was right up there with sex. To sit down and have burger after burger brought to you!

Pattye: Okay, between Floyd and the free burgers, what else could there possibly have been?

Scott: Truthfully, it was the fact that I never felt pressure to agree with you. You did not create an environment where I or anyone else for that matter was afraid to offer up a counter point of view. As we write this book and I reflect on other people I have worked with, you really did stand out. Your position of not caring who the idea came from, as long as it was a good idea, was a rare trait.

Pattye: Thank you. I appreciate that. Of course, I might add that you were never one to hold back if you didn't agree with me.

Scott: Eventually I held back because you would get this look that said: "Heard you, now stop."

Pattye: You caught that look, huh? I always wondered if you did.

Scott: It's like the one you are giving me now.

It's surprising how much you can accomplish if you don't care who gets the credit.

—Abraham Lincoln

If people think their opinions don't count, they quickly figure out it's just easier not to think. We can think of no faster way to ruin a company.

—Scott and Pattye

Corner Office Instinct 4

Take Pride in Sharing the Spotlight

Share (v.): divide equally among people

The "Credit Stealer" Manager

This boss loves taking credit for her (his) staff's work as her (his) own. When the going gets tough, she (he) finds one of her (his) staff to blame even if it is her (his) fault. The Credit Stealer is a master at deceiving her (his) superiors into thinking that she (he) is brilliant. She (he) manipulates every good outcome to make it look like she (he) initiated it. She (he) never gives credit. This boss is dangerous since you can get fired if she (he) thinks it will save her (his) job.

The "Criticizer" Manager

This boss doesn't like any ideas. He (she) only likes his (her) own. If you have a creative approach or a different way of doing something or a new suggestion, the criticizer will knock you down. He (she) has never heard an idea he (she) likes that wasn't his (her) own.

His (her) mission is to disagree with anything that is said. He (she) likes to be right, no matter what. The Criticizer will never give you positive feedback, but will always jump on your mistake. His (her) favorite saying is "Bad idea."

—Bossbitching.com (accessed December 2006)

We find these definitions of management styles both innovative and surprisingly accurate at the same time. They represent two examples of what often happens with the first major promotion up that corporate ladder. Over and over, we have noticed that with a promotion to a management position, new managers suddenly lose all sense of what is right and wrong. They probably got promoted because they had strong instincts, but they quickly allowed the instincts outlined in this book to evaporate. They become consumed with finding their way, and their way alone, into the spotlight. As a result, they begin to emulate the characteristics of the Criticizer and the Credit Stealer.

They become meticulous at finding ways to merchandise themselves and quick to discredit or demean those who provide no value to their career path; they view the talent pool of peers as competition rather than as a learning ground and as a place to find their corporate soul mate. Due to either their own insecurity or lack of self-awareness, they become the kind of managers no one wants to work for. They disregard the instincts of leadership and redirect the focus on themselves. This is why they don't like to share the spotlight. What they fail to see is that those they are leading don't like to always be left in the dark. Be aware and don't let this happen to you.

In our collective 50+ years in corporate America (the majority of that time was spent climbing the proverbial corporate ladder), if we told you how many times we were exposed to insecure managers like the Credit Stealer and the Criticizer, you would stand in awe. This insecurity is not the sign of damaged or hurtful character traits; instead, we believe it is the sign of individuals not understanding the role of a leader. It is also a sign that somewhere along the way they gained a warped perspective that everything generated from their team must be directly attributed back to them. In meetings, they take potshots at the ideas of others because they are under some misguided notion that destroying the initiative and ideas of others is the same as providing effective ideas. There has yet to be a building constructed by the wrecking ball. The wrecking ball has one purpose: to destroy. Ironically, this insecurity in leaders creates a human wrecking ball that can destroy the corporate environment they so desperately seek to maintain and to lead.

We know you are probably thinking that this is crazy and out-of-whack. It is, but welcome to corporate America where this happens every day.

We fondly refer to the collective impact of these traits as *me-i-tis. Surgeon general warning:* Promotions are known to cause severe cases of me-i-tis.

Me-i-tis is a slowly penetrating disease that will (and should) choke off any hope of moving up and advancing to the corner office. Please seek immediate help if you notice any of the following signs:

- You stop listening to other's ideas because they are not yours.
- You are reluctant to hire exceptional talent for fear they may surpass you.
- You have lost the ability to objectively discuss an alternative to your point of view.
- You view a discussion of *your* recommendations as a slight form of insubordination.
- You are more focused on being the author of an idea, rather than the intellectual observer and facilitator of great ideas.
- You limit exposure of sharp work associates to upper management because you think it could have a negative impact on your own advancement.

Although we're having some tongue-in-cheek fun with *me-i-tis,* it actually is a serious problem in corporate America. Whether you label it narcissism, paranoia, or insecurity, it is all grounded in a disillusioned sense of self-importance and a screwed-up value system. We have both worked with bosses, clients, and peers who have succumbed to the disease, and (confession time) we know that we have shown symptoms at times as well. What we've observed is that smart, successful people often succumb to this disease as they move up the corporate ladder. The higher up you go, the more susceptible you are.

Why is that? We believe it's partly because you start to believe your own press. If you're a rising star, you will receive a lot of praise for your ideas, your leadership, or your solution to a problem. In many cases, it will seem as if your efforts alone fuel your success. It is pretty easy for even the smartest people to start believing that they have the best ideas—after all, that's what everyone is telling them.

Fast Trackers Beware

One thing that I began to notice quite frequently once I was in senior management was the habit of the young up-and-comers to answer any question that came up—whether they had the answer or not. I remember sitting down with one of the brightest young minds I had ever worked with and asking him if I could give him some advice. I told him that just answering a client's question is not where you get the kudos. It's when you answer the question correctly that you get kudos. Unfortunately, this young man took it as a professional insult if he didn't have the answer. You see this time and time again, but it's a hard lesson to learn. Saying "I don't know" adds credibility to your other responses. You truly gain the respect of others if you say, "I don't have the answer to that, but I will get back to you."

—*Scott*

Are You Strolling Down the Street Naked?

Remember the story of the emperor who had no clothes? He was naked, but no one dared tell him otherwise. Unfortunately, there are many naked leaders out there. There are two big reasons you don't want to be a naked leader. First, it's just not pretty. (We both just looked in the mirror and we have to agree with the "not pretty" reason.) Second, to lead a team of "yes-people" is not the fastest way to get to the corner office. The fastest way to get to the corner office and to become a truly great leader is to encourage dissonant views, celebrate risk-taking, and always welcome open and honest dialogue. In doing so, you will have utilized the most important resources available to you—namely, the people working with you. When you have accomplished this, you will never be without clothes.

Truly great leaders learn to embrace debate and discussion. It is from debate and discussion that better ideas are formulated. The concept of "don't question me, I'm the leader" has the potential to ultimately destroy a company.

You do not need to be the author of every idea that comes from your group. Instead, your job as a leader is to encourage and nurture those ideas and to help others develop and make them better.

Management by Squirt Gun

In one of my first jobs out of college, I had a boss who truly valued and insisted on getting ideas from everyone who worked for him. I must admit that his method was a little extreme, but it certainly made a lasting impression on me. The first time I rushed into his office to tell him about a problem, he calmly opened his desk drawer, took out a water pistol, and shot me in the shoulder. I was stunned as I looked at the water running down my jacket. This executive proceeded to tell me that he wasn't paying me for problems—he was paying me for solutions and ideas. He told me he didn't care if my solution was the best one or the right one, but any time I brought him a problem, I needed to bring solutions as well. If not, I could expect to be shot. This really added new meaning to the phrase shooting the messenger. What a wise leader he was because he created an atmosphere where everyone was expected to contribute and where all ideas were valued.

—Pattye

We know from experience, however, that this instinct doesn't come naturally to most leaders and hard-charging potential leaders. You have to be keenly aware of this tendency and work like crazy to overcome it.

To help with that, we've identified four traits you want to avoid. Take the time to do an honest self-assessment. If you exhibit these traits, you have some work to do to hone this instinct.

Four Behavioral Traits That Will Lead to a Bad, Bad Case of Me-I-Tis

1. Ensuring That the Spotlight Stays on Me

This behavioral trait is the one responsible for a high level of office politics. We can all recognize someone who has this trait. It's the person in the meeting who always talks even when she has nothing to contribute. It's the person who cuts other people off before they even finish outlining their ideas and redirects the group to her idea or point of view. It's the person who is the first to shoot down other ideas. This person has zero listening skills and is only interested in one thing—getting credit.

2. Being the World's Greatest Firefighter (But Only Because You Are the Greatest Fire Starter)

There is no greater sign of insecurity than feeling as though your worth is defined by the problems you solve. We all know people who live by that motto. They come galloping to the rescue any time there is a fire, and they let everyone know that they just solved a *major* problem or prevented a *major* disaster. If you look closely, though, you'll often find a flaw with this. The flaw is that these firefighters are often creating problems and merchandising shortcomings to management *only* so they can later position themselves as the heroes in solving the problem. Unfortunately, disengaged senior managers often fall for this trick. So beware—this trait might get you promoted, but you won't have many loyal followers because your peers and subordinates can see right through you.

3. Hiring below Expectations Rather Than above Expectations

It is easy to say you subscribe to the theory of hiring the best athlete available, but it is another thing to actually do it. This trait alone is what ends the careers of many aspiring leaders. As you move up, you are only as good as the people who work for you. That bears repeating. You are only as good as the people who work for you. Powerful organizations are created because someone somewhere had the courage to hire people better than himself.

There's a famous story about advertising agency pioneer David Ogilvy that says it best. When someone was made head of an office, he would send them a Matrioshka doll from Gorky. Inside each was a smaller doll, and when the recipient opened the smallest doll the following message was discovered: *If each of us hires people who are smaller than we are, we shall become a company of dwarfs. But if each of us hires people who are bigger than we are, we shall become a company of giants.*

4. *Viewing Dialogue and Debate on Your Point of View as Corporate Treason*

Viewing debate as treasonous tends to appear once you have made it to a management position. Once again, it's not hard to identify someone who exhibits this behavior. This person gets angry when someone questions his opinion or challenges his ideas. It's easy to fall into the trap of believing that your associates are looking for firm direction (and they probably are), but they are looking for something more. They are looking for the opportunity to contribute, to be challenged, and to be heard.

Being a Leader Doesn't Mean You Have All the Answers

The hardest thing to get used to as president and CEO was the fact that when you were in an internal meeting, most considered you to be the smartest in the room simply because of your title. The best leader is not necessarily the smartest person in the room but the person who possesses the ability to create order and consensus out of chaos. I *welcomed* it when someone pushed back on a suggestion I put up for consideration. As a result, I started to remain silent at the start of meetings and tried to serve as the catalyst for discussion, posing "what ifs." A leader's job is to create more leaders and, to this day, I believe people grew from those discussions.

—Scott

Conclusion

Pay close attention to any reticence to share the spotlight as you move up the corporate ladder. If you find yourself controlling the discussion and discover that there is no discussion, stop, drop, and roll. Take a deep breath, and vow to listen and to invite ideas. It may take a couple of times for people to believe you, but you can—and must—change this trait if you want to be a great leader.

Five Questions to Ask Yourself to See if You Have the Instinct of Sharing the Spotlight

1. Do you find yourself getting excited when you hear an idea and immediately begin thinking how it could work?
2. When you're in a meeting or, more important, leading a meeting, do you make sure you get the opinions of everyone in the room?
3. Do you take time to ask questions and really listen to anyone who may be affected by a decision?

4. Do you remember what it feels like to have someone else take credit for your idea?
5. Have you ever hired anyone better or smarter than you?

If you didn't honestly answer yes to all of these questions, you may have me-i-tis. The good news is you can be cured. Read on.

Five Steps to Develop the Instinct of Sharing the Spotlight

1. Make a conscious effort in every meeting you lead or attend to ask for everyone's opinions. To make sure it happens, put it on the agenda.
2. Ask a trusted colleague or friend (a corporate soul mate, maybe?) to alert you if you're not listening or are too quickly shooting down other ideas.

A colleague and I had a secret code word that we used in meetings. We said it if the other person was becoming a bully and squashing ideas.

—Pattye

3. Schedule specific meetings with different levels of employees or customers simply to listen to their ideas.
4. Learn to ask the question: "What would you do if you were in my position?"
5. Post a big sign in your office that says "NO HUNTING." When people ask what it means, explain that there will be *no* shooting of messengers. If that was a bad habit of yours, own up to it, and tell them there is a new policy now. You want and need open feedback—good and bad. Here's a word of caution: If you want your corner office to have windows, you had better deliver on this.

5 Check for Blocked Arteries

SCOTT: I think the fact that I was single really helped me connect with my staff as I became president of the organization.

PATTYE: And how was that? Are you saying that if you were married you would not have been as effective of a leader?

SCOTT: Possibly not. The advertising agency business is a young person's business—a lot of young, single folks. As a result, when we had staff events, the hours got late, and it was easy for me to stay with the troops, have another beer, and talk about who knows what. I guarantee you that it wasn't work that endeared me to members of the staff.

PATTYE: You know, as ridiculous as that sounds, it makes sense.

SCOTT: Yeah, I think it was easy for me to look at those at the company as my extended family—not just in hollow words, but sincerely. I think they knew they were important to me, in a way that was different from others they have worked for. Because we are talking about taking things personally, there is one thing I want you to know—an observation on our 12-year relationship that this chapter has caused me to consider.

Pattye: What's that?

Scott: Not once during the first five years of our working relationship do I remember ever having a conversation regarding anything to do with my life. We talked for hours at night, on weekends, and traveled together. Yet, we never dedicated a portion of that time to an extended conversation about what was going on in my life. I find that fascinating.

Pattye: I don't—you didn't seem that interesting at the time.

I don't care how much you know until I know how much you care.

—Anonymous

Real leadership is about not being afraid to show that you care. People work harder for people they like and respect.

—Scott and Pattye

Corner Office Instinct 5

It's Okay to Take It Personally

Personal (adj.): relating to somebody's private life

Gallup's research shows that employees perform better for bosses who care about them. "The best organizations build caring work environments," write Kenneth A. Tucker and Vandana Allman in a Gallup Management Journal *article, "Don't Be a Cat-and-Mouse Manager." Tucker and Allman added, "They do this by encouraging managers to develop strong, nurturing relationships with their employees."*

How many times have you heard someone say, "Don't take it personally; it's just business." Well, it should come as no surprise that we couldn't disagree more. Think about it. Business *is* personal. Your career *is* personal. How you manage others *is* personal. To think and to act otherwise is to fool yourself and to shortchange your own career (as well as the careers of those who work for you).

Let us be perfectly clear here. When we say it's okay to take it personally, we don't mean it's acceptable to carry on in an unprofessional manner and to disregard any sense of workplace decorum. That doesn't work unless your corner office looks suspiciously like a playpen. When we say it's okay to take it personally, we mean it's permissible to take the wall down between your personal life and your professional life, and let others see your human side. We mean it's not only okay, but also highly recommended to take a personal interest in the lives of your colleagues and employees. It's okay to be genuine and to display real emotion. It's okay to care about more than the bottom line. And, if the time calls for it, it is okay to cry. In other words, taking it personally is about leading from the heart.

There's No Crying in Business: Wanna bet?

I ran a large local fast-food account in a rather large city. We had been handling the business for several years, and the time had come for the headquarters (two hours away) to resign this business. It was the primary business I worked on and the reason I had moved there. The head of the office asked me to resign the business at the next co-op meeting. The morning of the meeting, I went into another supervisor's office to practice my speech. Well, I got a quarter of the way through the speech and just broke down, sobbing like a baby in her arms. She knew how much I had enjoyed those people and what a labor of love I had put into their account. This emotional display had little to do with dollars and cents, but was the result of the human capital I had put in on their account and how I got to know many of them as friends. There are a handful of times I can remember crying in the office. It's odd, but it felt good to be so personally invested in something that caused such an emotional release.

—*Scott*

This is an instinct that is hard to teach, but it is critical in leadership because it lets those around you see a side of you that many leaders don't believe they can or should show. Assuming other instincts are present (and are able to serve as a check and balance), we see this personal investment as a good thing.

Learning from the Masters

Craig Abbott. Chuck Harrison. Jack Hartnett. Bobby Merritt. In our Sonic world, these gentlemen were masters of the universe. They were some of Sonic's largest and most successful franchisees. They were great operators, savvy businessmen, and good franchisees. But they also had something else in common—they cared deeply about their employees and their business. They wore their emotions on their sleeves—that is, when they had sleeves. They would literally give you the shirt off their backs. And we mean literally. Once a customer told one of them how much he liked the Sonic shirt he had on. Within minutes, the franchisee was wearing another shirt and the startled customer was holding the Sonic shirt.

It wasn't unusual to see these big men cry with joy or sadness about events in the lives of their employees. The times they each got involved personally in their employees' lives are too numerous to mention, but they bailed people out, literally, financially and emotionally. They gave second chances to people others wouldn't give a first chance to. They gave their hearts and what they got in return was respect, devotion, and success—not just personally, but for their businesses and their employees. We were so fortunate to learn about leading from the heart from these men (and many other franchisees we haven't mentioned here as well). If you can lead with your heart in the cut-throat fast-food business, you can lead with your heart anywhere.

—*Scott and Pattye*

Do They Know You Care?

Most of us probably spend more time at work than we do at home—which means we interact more, share more, challenge more, and rely more on our colleagues than we do on those at home (assuming there is someone at home). For the worker who is single, the work world often provides the sense of human interaction and dependence that makes him or her feel complete. It is not unusual to feel as though the office is where your family is housed.

In other words, you have an extended family at work. What you do *with* them determines what you get *out* of them.

Both of us believe there are positives that come from taking a genuine interest in the lives of your bosses, your peers, and your subordinates. When you take an interest in those around you, your leadership style takes on qualities that are meaningful, endearing, and supportive.

We believe that the more you understand those around you, the more you are able to effectively manage and motivate them. You will be amazed at what goes on in the mind of an employee when you sit down with her and let her share with you an accomplishment of a son or a daughter. It sends the message that you care about your employees beyond the value they bring to the office or to the corporate spreadsheet. You should have a genuine interest in their happiness and feel like a proud parent when they reach a new level of achievement at the office.

You would be amazed at the power of stopping in someone's office and asking him about his family. It's as simple as just taking 10 minutes and connecting with him as a person. Very quickly, he opens up and begins to share. In the long run, he won't forget it, and he will appreciate both the time and the thought you put into asking about his family. Where else can you get that kind of return for 10 minutes worth of conversation?

Makes It All Worth It

The following excerpts are from several notes that Scott received from employees and former employees over the years:

> Your leadership, passion, and sense of humor are unmatched. I've never met a person that could continually raise the bar, and do so in a motivating way.
>
> You always treated me as you did everyone with courtesy and respect. It meant a great deal.
>
> You have a genuine energy that few people possess.
>
> You were the key reason we enjoyed working at the agency so much. You are who made it a great place to work, and it wasn't just because of your business smarts. A lot of it had to do with your personality and approachability, from the funny comments at staff

meetings to the times when you just sat down in our cubicles and talked (sincerely talked). This made you a person instead of a president, and that made a huge difference. Others have tried to repeat, but the biggest difference was your sincerity. That can't be faked. I guess when you create a fun work atmosphere lead by people who truly care (like you did) the result is having more passionate and dedicated employees (like we were). Those were excellent years.

—*Scott*

These excerpts remind us of some advice given at the very early stages of our careers and we would like to share it with you. Regardless of what business you are in, as you move your way up the corporate ladder, you will (we hope) receive e-mails, letters or cards that thank you for something or acknowledge your efforts, your influence, your character, and more. Every time you receive one, we would ask that you put it in a file, not electronically, but print it out so you see it and feel it. You label that file "Warm and Fuzzy." You take it with you from office to office and job to job, adding to it at every stop.

And on those days (the ones we all have), when the business realities of the moment cause extreme self-doubt, stress or depression, you simply reach for the file. Lay the notes out on your desk and begin to read them one by one. Instantly, you are reminded why you love the business, the good others see in you and the impact you have had on associates. In no time, the negativity is minimized and your purpose reclaimed. This just might be the most important file you ever create and the only one with such medicinal power.

A Heart the Size of Texas

I had decided not to take the vice president job at Sonic even though I really liked the people and the company. I announced my decision to Dick Lear, a franchisee in Dallas with a heart bigger than Texas. He backed me up against the wall and proceeded to let me know that this was personal and that I would be letting him down if I didn't take it. In fact, he made me cry, and reconsider. I was so touched by how much he cared about the brand and about me that I decided I would take the job. Getting personal and showing that you care can make all the difference in the world. It did for me. Thank you, Dick.

—*Pattye*

We are not saying that every day at the office is like a five-hour therapy session. If you have this instinct, the interest and engagement with those around you comes naturally. There are moments (car rides, travel time, and meals) where you can connect on a completely different level. To get to the corner office, you must understand what is on the minds and in the hearts of those who depend on you.

This may be an instinct that some will take issue with; they will say you can't get personal and still make good business decisions. That may be true if you are Michael Corleone in *The Godfather,* who told Sonny: "It's not personal, Sonny. It's strictly business." (We're guessing that the dead guy thought it was personal, by the way!) We've certainly all worked for some "godfathers" out there, but that's not the right way to lead. We believe there may be no more selfish action from management than that of expecting all employees to check their lives at the elevator door.

We don't mind if employees take work home; we embrace and celebrate when associates take their nutcracker (see Chapter 9) home and solve problems. Yet, we have the audacity to expect them not to bring any of their home life to work? Doesn't seem quite fair, does it?

We've both been very fortunate to have worked for and with people who did take it personally and who showed a great interest in our lives. Because of that, we worked harder, we cared more, and we felt a deep sense of loyalty and pride. To help you understand just how important this is, we thought we'd share some things that have happened to us over the years that are wonderful illustrations of this:

Pattye Remembers

- I was on a business trip with a colleague and had my purse stolen at the airport. This gentleman and his associates felt so bad about it that they presented me with a brand new purse at our next meeting.
- As a new member of senior management, I was heartbroken when I learned that a board meeting had been scheduled at the same time as an important school concert. Because the chairman and CEO was so understanding, he had the board meeting rescheduled.
- When I went through an unexpected and sudden divorce, the chairman of the company I worked for took time to come visit with me personally. He closed the door, expressed his sympathy and compassion, and sincerely told

me to let him know if I needed anything. He also told me to take off whenever I needed to.

- As a single mom, I had no choice one day but to bring a toddler to work with me—just for a few hours. I situated her in the conference room across from my office—with Cheerios and a Barney video—checking on her every few minutes. Much to my surprise, I discovered that same chairman sitting in there and watching Barney with her. This wise grandfather and leader told me to quit worrying and get back to work; Melissa would be fine.

Scott Remembers

- The account I revealed earlier that I had to resign—well, the rest of the story is that the franchise group did not accept the resignation. They thought the fact that one of the two owners didn't have the guts to come down and resign it himself was a disgrace. They could see that I was being asked to do something (resign their business) that ultimately would result in my unemployment—and they wanted no part of it. They got on the phone, called Los Angeles and demanded the CEO come to San Diego. He did, and he got a lesson in leadership that he should have already learned.
- Working on an airline account, I was in London for the first time and had been working around the clock. On my last day there, the head of the office grabbed me, took me to a tour bus, and made me take a four-hour tour of the city so I could at least have some sense of appreciation of where I was.
- I was the honoree at a dinner to raise money for the Arthritis Foundation and my assistant helped coordinate the

surprise arrival from Florida of my parents. I had not seen them for quite some time, and to see them come walking in from the back of the room was really a memory that will last a lifetime.

Take Care with the Company You Keep

We've talked a lot about being emotionally involved with the *people* you work with. It is also healthy to become emotionally invested in something that you can't always control all aspects of—your company or brand.

Did you ever see a picture of a dejected fan sitting in his seat after the game? It's pretty clear that he took his team and the outcome of the game personally. Sports fans take this emotional investment to the extreme. They wear their team logo proudly, and they feel that logo allows them to be connected to something bigger that they don't control. Even though they don't control it, they emotionally reap the upside and downside of the team's performance. People like to be emotionally invested in things that are a big part of their lives, even if they have little control over the final performance.

Well, there is no reason that the company can't fill the emotional void of the home team.

Work is a big part of everyone's life. Make it your mission to help everyone (yourself included) be a fan for your company. Wear your company logo proudly and encourage others to do so as well. It provides an emotional connection, a sense of belonging, and a sense of pride. However, monitor your behavior while in corporate clothing. You are a walking advertisement for the brand. Many times while delayed in an airport, we have seen people drink more than they should—which results in obnoxious behavior both in the airport and on the plane—and there, larger than life, is their company logo plastered all over the front of their shirts. In this case, they are probably not good spokespeople for the brand.

Conclusion

If you are practicing this instinct, your enthusiasm will catch on. It will make work more fun, more productive, and more rewarding. To get personally involved with staffers or clients and to still be able to manage in the best interest of the organization is the ultimate display of corporate self-confidence and leadership.

Five Questions to Ask Yourself to See if You Have the Instinct of Taking It Personally

1. When someone who reports to you resigns, do you take a hard look at what you could have done differently?
2. Have you ever been to the house of a direct report for social reasons?
3. Do you ever stop by an office, sit down, and ask the associate how things are with the family?
4. When aware of issues, do you ever insist that associates not come in or take time off to deal with their issues?
5. Do you send birthday cards or holiday cards to associates and their spouses?

If you answered no to any of these questions, your heart may be getting hard. A proper diet and exercise as prescribed next should open those arteries in no time.

Five Steps to Develop the Instinct of Taking It Personally

1. Make it a point to take key direct reports to lunch over the next month and vow to not talk about business. Share some of your life and interests, and learn about theirs.
2. When someone has been working really long hours, send their spouse flowers or a dinner gift card with a note that says you noticed and appreciate the efforts.
3. If you know a colleague has a sick child or problems at home, yet they are buried with a big project, offer to help in ways that *won't* get noticed but will ease some of the burden.
4. Don't be afraid to show your emotions.
5. Remember the little things—kid's names, hobbies, and birthdays—even if you have to write them down.

6 I Rest My Case, Your Honor

Scott: I'm wanted for kidnapping, you know.

Pattye: Wait—what?

Scott: With the help of my management team, we kidnapped an entire office one day.

Pattye: There's a headline for your resume. How'd you manage that?

Scott: We told them a couple weeks beforehand to block off an afternoon, then we had four big buses out front of the office and made them all leave their desks and get their butts onto the buses.

Pattye: That must have been quite a ransom you were going for.

Scott: Nope—just the opposite. It was a "thank you" kidnapping. We took all the buses full of employees to the local mall. No one had any idea what was going on.

Pattye: Did anyone call the police?

Scott: Would you call the police if you and your colleagues were each handed $100 and told you had an hour to spend it?

Pattye: No, but I may have called in a psychiatrist.

Scott: Oh, it gets better. They had to spend the cash on themselves—not a spouse, not a child, not a boyfriend.

Pattye: What a great idea.

Scott: Not finished yet—

Pattye: Really?

Scott: That was just the warm up. We got them back on the buses, took them to a local club for drinks and some food. Then, at 5:00 P.M., they could stay or leave.

Pattye: So you did let them go—and how did they like being held hostage?

Scott: The buzz was amazing, not just in the office but throughout town. The local paper even ran a story on the event.

A man has honor if he holds himself to an ideal of conduct even when it is inconvenient, unprofitable, or dangerous to do so.

—Walter Lippmann, American journalist

Being the kind of leader your people can count on is often inconvenient and can be unprofitable.

—Scott and Pattye

Corner Office Instinct 6

Protect, Honor, and Defend Those Who Work for You

Protect (v.): look after, save from harm
Honor (v.): respect, revere
Defend (v.): support, stand up for

According to the latest national Gallup Management Journal *survey, happy employees are better equipped to handle workplace relationships, stress, and change. And no one plays a greater role in their well-being and engagement, the survey finds, than their supervisor.*

The day you begin to supervise even one other person you take on an enormous responsibility. This responsibility includes influencing, and often defining, a person's career, livelihood, family life, and even sense of self-worth.

When we supervised, our leadership was simple and clear—we vowed to always protect, honor, and defend those who worked for us. We found that placing them first, with these vows in mind, brought improved morale, strengthened performance, and increased retention—three areas any leader should strive to impact.

Note to the current or aspiring leader: Living this instinct is dependent on your ability to provide unconditional respect for those you manage. This respect includes the desire to always protect, honor, and defend your staff. In the business world, if your leadership does not protect, honor, and defend your people, what will? This instinct must govern your actions in both good times and bad. *Warning:* The bad times are the most challenging and require discipline. When times get tough in corporate America, the result is often a frenzy of pointing fingers and the search for scapegoats.

Do not allow this instinct to come in and out of your management practice. This instinct serves you well on the road to the corner office because it demonstrates to all that you are a leader who acts in a consistent, ethical manner, regardless of the environment. This instinct is about leading with a steady hand and upholding ethics and integrity *no matter what.*

Place People First

There was a time when business was flat and our company had an abusive client. The team traveled across the country to attend meetings and then they were berated and treated with little, if any, respect. After hearing story after story like this, management reached the tough decision to resign the client. This hurt the company's profitability and every employee's share value in the short term. When I announced it, however, they applauded. To this day, I believe they applauded the decision because they saw management placing a value on the employee that exceeded that of the almighty dollar. That is how you lead with this instinct.

—Scott

Do You Have What It Takes to Always Protect, Honor and Defend?

Protect: Take the Heat for Those Who Burn Easily

Nothing will earn you more respect or endearment from those who work for you than the concept of *protect.*

Protect means you serve as a barrier—a bulletproof vest of sorts—when it comes to attacks on your staff. Your people need to know that, as their leader, you start with unconditional trust and faith in their efforts and intent. This instinct delivers a safe and secure environment to them.

When leaders blend the best qualities of a coach, mentor, professor, and parent, they are viewed as the kind of leader who will always protect the interests of their associates. In return, the following things will happen:

- The associates will be more productive because they won't be worried about protecting themselves. Research shows that productivity can increase up to 40 percent if workers feel secure with their job and work environment.
- Issues will be brought up promptly in a trustful and blameless environment.
- Innovation will flourish as risks are rewarded, not punished.

If you protect your employees, you create a low-risk environment where people feel free to share ideas, suggest new and innovative ideas, and even (gasp!) dare to criticize or challenge the status quo. People need the assurance that these ideas will be received in the spirit they were offered—even if the ideas are not workable or the critique is not flattering. A low-risk environment lets everyone participate fully without fear of censure; it allows risk-taking and cutting-edge thinking; and it really encourages employees to make an emotional and intellectual investment in their jobs or company.

Ideas Welcome Here

Some companies get it. They encourage risk-taking, and they welcome ideas from all employees. QuikTrip Corporation, a convenience store and gasoline retailer, is one of those companies. They exemplify a low-risk environment and leadership who welcomes all ideas. I recently observed this openness to input during an audit committee meeting where potential accounting firms were being interviewed. A very competent administrative assistant, Kandy Collins, was responsible for getting all the proposals in and for making the arrangements for the presentations. As a result, she had a great deal of contact with the firms.

On the day of the presentations to the audit committee and senior management, Kandy was there to take notes. At the end of the presentations, when we were discussing the pros and cons of the various firms, Kandy offered her observations and comments. In most corporate boardrooms, that would not happen. I was surprised, but thrilled because she had very good observations. I looked around the room while she was talking to check out the reactions of senior management, and there was no adverse reaction. It was obvious that this was a perfectly normal thing to happen. Kandy seemed very comfortable being able to contribute, but why wouldn't she? The current CFO, Sandi Westbrook, started her QuikTrip career as an accounting clerk/

errand girl, so it's pretty clear that contributions are welcome at any level and recognized and rewarded. I commented on how remarkable this was to Chet Cadieux, the chairman and CEO, and he was surprised that I thought it was out of the ordinary. It's quite evident that he gets the concept of protect and has created a low-risk environment where all ideas are welcome. Maybe that's why QuikTrip has been on the Fortune 100 Best Places to Work list for the past five years.

—*Pattye*

Every single day you have endless opportunities to develop and demonstrate this instinct. Every decision, every comment, how you resolve conflict, even body language during a meeting—all of these convey to your staff whether you are about "them," or just about "you."

Walk on Fire

We had a client who completely understood this instinct. She was the head of marketing and, as such, had final approval over the television commercials that we produced. She encouraged us to take risks and protected us fiercely when we did. I'll always remember one occasion in particular when we presented a finished spot that, quite frankly, just didn't work. No one liked it and everyone was trying to figure out ways to fix it.

After multiple revisions, she simply said, "Kill it. It doesn't work. Sometimes that happens. Don't worry about it—I approved it so we're in this together. Let's figure out what else we can do." Other clients would have ranted, raved, and demanded that we eat the cost while developing complete amnesia about the approval process.

Her gesture alone would have been enough for the creative folks to walk on fire for her. However, the story doesn't stop there. She ultimately faced criticism for this failure. When someone demanded to know who was responsible, her answer was simple. She replied, "I was. I approved it." Our team went from willing to walk on fire to willing to eat fire for her. What was her name? Pattye.

—Scott

This *does not* mean you blindly protect and ignore poor performance. In those cases, you act swiftly to minimize the damage. By doing so, you are actually protecting those on your team who are carrying their own weight *and* adding that of the underperformers.

Here are some tips to help you develop the *protect* aspect of this instinct:

- Consistently demonstrate disapproval of those who blatantly seem to be out for themselves. Do not reward their behavior with plum assignments, even if it will make your life easier in the short term.
- Never point your finger. When there is a mistake, do not start with, "Who is responsible for this?" Instead ask, "How do we fix this and keep it from happening again?"
- Stand up and take the heat in public. Then, in private, remedy the situation.
- When you have to reprimand (and you will have to), never do it in public or via e-mail or voice mail. Protect your

workers by taking the more effective route—face-to-face behind closed doors.

- Reward mistakes that come from taking risks.

Honor: Care and Compassion Are Not Only Good Hospital Words; They Are Exceptional Management Words

It's not enough to protect your employees. You must truly care about them as people. Unfortunately, corporate America is not known for its care and compassion. That is good news because it gives you a wonderful opportunity to be different—to be a *real* leader.

We both genuinely cared about the people who worked for us, and they knew it. The word *care* can be trite at times. However, we were never afraid to show our appreciation for people's efforts and dedication.

While we both may have honored our staff more than most, we were careful not to allow this genuine caring to cloud the tough issues that faced us as managers every day. A tough balancing act was needed to ensure *honor* was practiced in a positive way.

We all know managers who are consumed by people's opinions of them and avoid the tough decisions. That's not what this instinct is about. Compassion did not keep us from making hard decisions like department reorganizations, layoffs, or pay freezes—even if it impacted friends or staff we had become close with. When your staff knows they are genuinely cared for, these tough decisions are greeted with respect and an understanding that a particular action was in the best interest of all.

Business Is Business

Twice, I had to let people go who were very close to me. One time it was one of my closest friends. While others in management kept asking if it was something I really had to do, I stayed true to the best interests of the company and didn't waver because it was something that had to be done. It did cause me sleepless nights, but friendship is not a reason to make exceptions. If I had, I would have sent the wrong message to everyone and created questions regarding my leadership. Instead, the message to everyone was clear: I would not waver in making decisions that were in the best interest of the company, even when they were difficult to make on a personal level.

—*Scott*

Honoring your associates will come naturally when you care about them. As you move up and find yourself managing staff or adding to the staff you manage, accomplishments will, in large part, be due to their efforts, not yours. There are no gestures too small when it comes to celebrating success.

A great example of honor was demonstrated by the coach of the 2005 World Series Champions, the Chicago White Sox. When they won, the players celebrated on the field while the coach sat back and watched. When asked why he didn't run out of the dugout to join the players, he explained, "They played the game; they won—this is about them."

Even at an Awards Ceremony, It's about the Team

I've had the good luck to work with many great and humble leaders and to observe how they run their companies. David Kyle, who is the chairman of the board of ONEOK, a Fortune 500 energy company, has a reputation as a leader who focuses first and foremost on his team. I saw that in action at a recent awards ceremony where David was inducted into the Tulsa Hall of Fame, along with several other prominent Tulsans. Each winner had someone who introduced him or her and talked about his or her accomplishments, and then the winner spoke. The person who introduced David didn't talk about David's accomplishments. (I suspect that David urged him to speak instead about the growth and the accomplishments of ONEOK's employees over the years.) David's remarks were also entirely about the employees of ONEOK and what ONEOK has accomplished. There was nothing about him. That was in stark contrast to the other award winners, whose introductions and remarks were about them. But, that's how David leads—it's not about him. It's about his team.

—*Pattye*

Here are some tips to help you develop the *honor* aspect of this instinct:

- Drop in on your staff and ask how things are going "outside the office." Inquire about personal achievements or accomplishments made by other family members.
- Personalize anniversary letters and send them to the employee's home address.

- Send birthday, Mother's Day, and Father's Day cards to the spouses of your staff acknowledging that efforts given at the office often require sacrifices at home.
- Send flowers or a gift certificate to the spouse of someone who has been working extended hours or traveling frequently.
- When success occurs, highlight and salute the smallest of contributions, and downplay the positions with seniority.
- Look for reasons to thank, salute, and congratulate associates for their efforts.

Defend: Work *with* Your Direct Reports as Both a Leader and a Member of the Team

No one advances in corporate America today, much less makes it to the corner office, *on his or her own.* The *defend* instinct is demonstrated by conveying to your staff that you think of yourself as a member of their team.

You want to be seen as the coach who is in the dugout with them, not as the general manager who sits in the office constantly evaluating their worth. Coaches who connect with and stand up for their players often get maximum results.

How does this translate to the workplace? If you hide in your office spending all your time managing up, you will not be relating to your staff and eventually you will be deemed an ineffective leader. You won't have a clue as to what your people are doing, what challenges and obstacles they are facing, who sits where, and how the work even gets done. If you don't know those things, you can't very well protect them and you certainly won't be in a position to honor them.

The Parade

Being visible and involved makes such a difference. I remember (with pride) one time when I was at a franchisee's convention in New Orleans during the month of July. It was hot, steamy, and miserable, and we were part of a marching band parade—Mardi Gras style—through the streets. I started talking to the gentleman next to me and learned that he had recently joined Sonic from Burger King. When he learned that I was the president of Sonic, he was totally astonished. He said he couldn't believe I was there with them, marching and sweating. He said he had worked for Burger King for 18 years and had never even met a vice president. My thought was what a loss—not his, but theirs.

—*Pattye*

Make the commitment to defend your people. In doing so, you reinforce the message that no *one* person is more or less important in a team. To be successful at this you must make an effort to build a genuine connection between you and your staff—and sometimes, most importantly, the most junior member of your staff. As you move up, most will expect you to increasingly distance yourself from lower-level employees and it will be easy to do so, given the demands on your time. Here's another chance, though, to stand out and be a different type of leader. Stay in touch with all your employees. You can't defend that which you don't know or understand.

Here are some tips to help you develop the *defend* aspect of this instinct:

- Jump in to help on occasion. Stay late to help them put a presentation together. Make sure, however, that you're being helpful—not just gumming things up.
- Ask before leaving if there is anything you can do to help—and mean it.
- Be accessible and available to all your staff and interested in the issues they are concerned with. Do you remember how you valued the time you had with your bosses when you were starting out?
- Encourage any positive, well-meaning critiques of the status quo—so much that no one is afraid of retribution for coming to you with suggestions.
- Always be honest and share as much as you can; honesty is a strong link to developing trust.

Conclusion

Take a Leadership Oath

Jurors are sworn in. Elected officials take an oath of office. Boy Scouts recite a pledge. Couples exchange marriage vows with each other.

We have one simple question: Why isn't there a leadership oath of office? You will be an ineffective leader if no one follows you, and *very* few will passionately follow a leader who does not take an oath to protect, honor, and defend their charges. If you are going to lead, you need to take this oath as seriously as any of the other oaths.

When you first get an opportunity to manage, we suggest doing the following exercise—it is one that could change your professional life forever: Go home, pour a glass of wine (or the beverage of your choice), turn on some music, and grab a pen and paper. Ask yourself one simple question: "What personality traits and style would you want in your next boss?"

When you are done, look at the list. Make a vow with yourself that you will work to deliver those traits to your first direct report.

Senior management looks to promote those who can rally the troops—who can get them focused and motivated to achieve goals. If you are going to ascend to the corner office, you must be able to not only articulate a compelling vision and direction, but you must also find a way to emotionally and personally connect with those who will be working for you. Your direct reports will depend on your leadership and *you* will depend on their quality of work. Your success in getting to the corner office will be directly linked to your ability to motivate your associates to achieve a quality of work second to none.

Five Questions to Ask Yourself to See if You Have the Instinct to Protect, Honor, and Defend

1. Have you ever taken the blame or criticism for something someone on your team did?
2. Can you remember the last time you stayed late with the troops to help on a project?
3. Have you ever done something special for an employee who has been working extra hours?
4. Do you avoid asking "Who is responsible?" or "Who made that mistake?" and focus on "How do we fix this and keep it from happening again?"
5. Do you spend any time with the lowest paid associate on your team?

If you answered yes to all the above, congratulations! You know how to protect, honor, and defend; your employees will help you move up. If not, focus on developing this instinct by taking the following actions.

Five Steps to Develop the Instinct to Protect, Honor, and Defend

1. Implement an evaluation process where your direct reports evaluate you (anonymously) and probe them about the issues of protect, honor, and defend.
2. Hire a life coach to help you implement specific exercises at work to engage on a deeper level with your staff.
3. Every six months, commit to sending each member of your staff a thank-you card for their efforts on behalf of the company. Send this card to the employee's home and specifically refer to something he or she has done over and above his or her normal job.
4. Have lunch with someone different on your staff every week, just the two of you.
5. Find a reason to celebrate as a staff every four months.

7 9 *to* 5 Was Just a Movie

SCOTT: So, Pattye, when did *it* start for you?

PATTYE: As usual, I'm a couple of steps behind you. Which *it?*

SCOTT: You know, the *it* in *itch,* as in the itch to work harder, do more, or volunteer to take on extra projects. But why am I asking? I bet you were an overachiever in preschool.

PATTYE: No way did I start that early! It wasn't until much later—say, kindergarten—that I started volunteering to help the teacher. What about you?

SCOTT: Can't say that I started in kindergarten, but I know that by the time I was a resident advisor in college, I figured out that when you're responsible for or to other people, you don't have a quitting time.

PATTYE: That reminds me of the saying "Leaders don't quit; quitters don't lead."

SCOTT: It reminds me that I'm tired and need a nap.

Nothing takes the place of persistence.

—Ray Kroc

Persistence never asks what time it is.

—Scott and Pattye

Corner Office Instinct 7

Jobs Have Time Clocks—Careers Don't

> **Career** (n.): a field for or pursuit of consecutive, progressive achievement, especially in public, professional, or business life

> *According to a study by Booz Allen Hamilton, the top 50 traditional NYSE company CEOs put in 60 to 65 hours a week.*

We never told you the road to the corner office was short. You might be able to avoid putting in such long hours if your dad owns the company, but if you want to arrive at the corner office, you had best be prepared for what awaits you behind the door. It's an indisputable fact that Americans work more than any other industrialized nation, and we can tell you from personal experience that leaders and aspiring leaders are driving that average up.

Don't let the hours the CEO works frighten you. You need to accept that it will take at least that amount of time and probably more to demonstrate you have what it takes to get to that office. Yes, unfortunately in many cases, it takes more than 60 to 65 hours a week. But it is not all doom and gloom. The long hours required hardly become an issue if you have a soul mate, a passion for what you do, and the proper leadership instincts. But make no mistake about it: to get to the corner office, you must be aware of, accept, and embrace the hours needed for the journey.

This chapter is designed to filter out those who are weak of heart for long nights with bad Chinese food at the office. There is a politically correct movement afoot that finds many in the workforce taking the opposite approach. They work fewer hours and generate more time for themselves or for others. It is a choice each individual makes. Some choose to deemphasize their career and make it more of a job, something they can leave at the end of the day and not revisit until they sit at their desks the next day. Others (we presume those who are reading this book) want to grab all they can, and create a career with unlimited potential, and they recognize that the hours are going to be different. People who love what they do and are genuinely engaged, curious, and eager to learn never stop working. There is a different term for these folks—*fast tracker.*

Fast trackers have that *itch* to do more, to learn more, and to help out, and they feel responsible *to* or *for* people. As a result, they don't pay attention to time. They pay attention to results, to people, and to their tasks. We have found that these aspiring leaders take that same approach whether it is at work, at church, or for the local theater group.

Arthritis Doesn't Wear a Watch

I've been involved with the national Arthritis Foundation for almost 20 years. Watching the tireless efforts of volunteers helped me understand the difference between workers and leaders early in my career. I saw people from all professions—doctors, lawyers, accountants, corporate chiefs (many struggling with arthritis)—work unbelievably long hours "volunteering" to help people with arthritis. Meetings lasted late into the night and all weekend. During those marathon sessions, people were eager, enthusiastic, energetic, and happy. Most of these folks also had big "real" jobs that required long hours as well. Why did they do this and how did they keep it up? The answers are love and passion (if you didn't know that, please reread Chapter 2).

—*Pattye*

Are You Looking at Your Watch, or Are You Looking Ahead?

We both discovered early in our careers that when you love what you do, going the extra mile is effortless. You will know you have emotionally committed to a career when you find yourself suddenly volunteering to stay late, taking on extra projects, and seldom, if ever, looking at your watch or wondering, "What time is it?"

You will work more hours and give up more weekends than anyone you know. And you will know you have developed the corner office instinct because it won't seem like a sacrifice. Just think of all the money you are saving by not going out.

The comment about sacrifice is a critical one. Make no mistake: getting to the corner office absolutely requires sacrifices. Working long hours and missing out on many a social outing *are* sacrifices. If you merely tolerate the hours, rather than embrace them and thrive on the product you are producing, you will be exposed just like a bad actor who can't find the motivation for a part. We advise against trying to fake your way through this one. If you volunteer begrudgingly to stay late and work on a project, you'll be sneaking a peek at that watch, commenting on what you gave up. This attitude will show in your demeanor and your work product.

If You Think Weekends Are Miller Time, Think Again

Both of us found that we used the weekends quite frequently as we rose in our careers. We used this time differently at various stages in our careers, but the weekend was invaluable in providing time to think and get real work done, but also (if we're honest) in giving us a platform to get us noticed.

The challenge early in our careers was attempting to demonstrate an impressive capacity for work as well as providing the bosses an impressive product. To demonstrate both work capacity and intellect, we discovered we needed an abundance of a hard-to-find currency—time.

This is where Saturday came in quite handy early in our careers.

The Saturday Stroll

We both liked to come into the office on Saturday. On Saturday, we marched into our offices at 10:00 A.M. in the hopes that someone, anyone, from senior management would see our cars in the parking lot or hear noise coming from our offices. I know you might be wondering why we mentioned noise. Where there was noise, there was the likelihood that a senior manager would follow his or her ears and eventually be standing in the doorway, offering up some quip about how tough it must be to be at work on Saturday. When that happened, you could almost smell the promotion coming. If the car and the noise had not produced a senior manager by 1:00 P.M., we resorted to the "Saturday

Stroll." If the bosses were not going to come to us, we went to them. This was our stage. Things did not always go as planned, and there was no more deflating feeling than heading home at 2:00 P.M. and realizing no one from senior management had been to the office that day.

Come on, you can admit it. You've done this, too. As senior management, however, we have to admit that we have tiptoed to our offices on Saturday so we could get some work done without having to spend time with all the "strollers." Some strollers don't understand the importance of brevity.

—*Scott*

Later in our careers, we found that the best, uninterrupted time to clear our minds and tackle some "extra projects" was still on a Saturday. Now be honest, if you winced a little or sighed out loud when you read the word Saturday, we need you to read it again. Read it a few more times until it doesn't hurt anymore. In time, you will learn to embrace Saturdays and view the time in the office as a step in the long journey to the corner office.

Weekend Warrior Redefined

As I moved into positions with more seniority, I actually came into the office on the weekends much less. Some of that was because of the changing nature of my work, and some was due to technology. But weekends were still important for thinking, catching up with trends, reading trade publications, assessing competitors, and tackling big projects. By not being in the office, though, I was able to weave work and family commitments together more effortlessly. After the soccer game, I might take the girls to McDonald's. The time together was good for them, and it was good for me to scope out what new things the competition was doing. And I'd quiz the girls on what they liked and didn't like. Watching television at night with the family gave me a chance to see what was new in the world of television programming and commercials. If you want to get to the corner office, you have to be thinking and learning, whether it's at night or on the weekend (see Chapter 9 for more on this). *Warning:* Too much of a good thing isn't always good for you (see Chapter 15 for more on this).

—Pattye

Conclusion

If you want to make it to the corner office and be a leader, then you have to put in the hours and do so eagerly and without resentment. Whether you come in on Saturday, stay late, volunteer to take on an extra project, or volunteer in the community, you will accomplish two things: First, you will be seen as someone who has what it takes to move up and who is willing to work hard. Second, and even more important, you'll learn something new about the business, forge new relationships, and have time to actually think (trust us, thinking is a good thing).

Five Questions to Ask Yourself to See if You Have the Instinct of *Career* versus *Job*

1. Do you feel anticipation in going to the office on a weekend because you know there are few, if any, distractions?
2. Are you willing to eat a dinner or two alone at the office?
3. Do you challenge your own capacity by taking on extra projects?
4. Is the task always more important than the time required to complete it?
5. Do you have friends who understand your drive at work and, as a result, who have a positive influence on you?

If you answered yes to all of the above, then you understand the difference between a career and a job.

Five Steps to Develop the Instinct of *Career* versus *Job*

1. Volunteer to stay late to help with a big project. *Hint:* A big project could be stuffing envelopes or putting labels on a mailer that needs to go out. There should be no project beneath you.
2. Step up to the plate in a meeting and offer to take on the task that has everyone else looking at their shoes—or, at least, offer to help with it.
3. Start going to the office on Saturdays to tackle "thinking" projects or to organize and clean. If you don't have enough of your own work, offer to help the overworked colleague in the next cubicle.

4. Go visit your competitors, or spend time researching information about them.
5. Volunteer. We mean really volunteer for some organization that you have a passion for—whether that's theater, working with kids, or a health charity.

II

Performance Instincts

8 Open 24 Hours

Scott: Even though I've never been married, sometimes it sure seemed like we were husband and wife.

Pattye: I'm afraid to ask why you say that.

Scott: Because your voice was the last thing I heard before I went to bed at night and the first thing I heard in the morning. Why do you suppose that was?

Pattye: Probably because you had an obsessive habit of checking your voice mail!

Scott: Only because you had an obsessive, and well-documented, habit of leaving voice mails at all hours of the night. But that habit came back to haunt you at a company Christmas party, didn't it?

Pattye: Yes, it did, and it showed behavior even more obsessive than ours. One year at our company Christmas party, the spouse of one of my coworkers came to me and asked me why I left her husband voice mails in the middle of the night and disrupted their sleep (emphasis on their).

Scott: I can't wait to hear how you answered her question.

Pattye: I was startled because it never occurred to me that my insomnia would be bothering anyone. I thought I was being efficient. So I asked her how she knew and why it was disruptive.

Scott: Do tell.

Pattye: Anyway, she explained that her husband had his voice mail connected to his pager. Any time he received a voice mail, his pager went off. He kept it on the nightstand and would get up and check his messages whenever it went off. I was so embarrassed that I stopped leaving messages in the middle of the night—for him, at least.

Scott: Okay, going to bed and getting up with you isn't that bad after all.

Pattye: My husband, Mark, would agree—I hope.

BUNNY: "Don't you think you'd better go? The tortoise has the lead."

MAX HARE: "Say, I've lots of time to play. My middle name is speed."

—"The Tortoise and the Hare," Aesop

The race to the corner office is a marathon, not a sprint. Slow and steady—and smart—beat speed in that race every time.

—Scott and Pattye

Corner Office Instinct 8

Smart Always Beats Fast

Smart (adj.): clever, shrewd, and calculating in business and other dealings

Technology is the drug of choice for most Americans.
—Source unknown

Aesop's fable of the tortoise and the hare is a perfect analogy for what technology has done to many smart business leaders. Technology has made them fast—just like the hare. But it has also lured them into believing that fast wins the race. Speed doesn't win in the fable, and it doesn't in corporate America. Smart always beats fast. Always.

Open 24 Hours Used to Be Just for Diners

With technology, people are now accessible 24/7. We have BlackBerries and Treos. We can get reception just about anywhere, and we can always check and respond to our e-mails. Because of that, an expectation now exists that people will respond immediately, no matter what.

We were probably lucky that, early in our careers, we didn't have the technology to be accessible 24/7. We actually had to drive our cars (gasp!) without talking on the phone or reading e-mails (is that crazy and dangerous, or what?). We're not so old that we had to handwrite letters and send them out via Pony Express, but we did have time to think about responses, and we often had to communicate in person or by phone (more on that increasingly rare form of communications later). We will confess, however, that when the technology did become available, we got caught up in the speed and efficiency of it all. We had to exercise exceptional discipline not to allow it to control our entire life (one of us was better at this than the other).

Proud to Be One of the Last Holdouts

As technology progressed, everyone at the agency was clamoring to get the new PDA that served as both phone and e-mail. When it came my turn, I refused. I felt as if the issue was similar to a separation of church and state. I told our vice president of information technology that I had no interest in having a phone that also served as my office inbox. I explained that when I make a call at a ballgame, or get a call on Saturday at 9:00 A.M., I don't want the temptation of looking at a screen that serves as the front door to my office. I knew the logic was old school, but I spent enough time in my office that I certainly didn't want the office with me *everywhere* I went. I'm sure they laughed at the antiquated logic, but knowing what I now know, I wouldn't have changed a thing.

—Scott

You may think that you are demonstrating unparalleled passion for the business by the lone fact that you are the fastest gun in the West. You may take great pride in the commitment to respond to e-mails and voice messages instantly. You are certain that the bigwigs will be impressed because they see that you're thinking about work even at 2:30 A.M. Guess what?

We're not impressed, and neither is your boss. Send us a message at 2:30 A.M. and we think you are drunk from a night out, you need to get a life, or you need a better mattress.

Did You Remember to Carbon Copy God?

A friend of mine confessed to me that he had gotten in big trouble with his wife over his new BlackBerry. It seems that he was checking messages in church. His wife noticed and reached over, punched him (rightly so), and made him stop. It's ironic, but since he told me that story, I've now noticed other people checking their messages during church as well. A word of caution, though, before you rush to judgment. I observed a pastor checking messages on his PDA during a sermon, and I was appalled, only to later learn that he had the Bible loaded and was actually looking up Bible verses.

—*Pattye*

It's so easy to become addicted to speed (not the drug, but that's true as well). Checking and responding instantly to messages truly becomes an addiction (ask spouses across America if you don't believe us), and you need to treat it as one. Here are some signs that you've become addicted to what we call *office speed:*

- You have read and sent an e-mail while you were behind the wheel of a car.
- You have a Pavlov-type response to that electronic "you've got mail" signal, and, no matter what you're working on, you stop and check your e-mail.
- Even worse, you not only stop and check it, but you fire off an instant response.
- You check for new messages constantly—at stoplights, ball games, the theatre—sometimes by covertly hiding your PDA in your lap.
- Your cell phone is always with you, and you always answer it no matter where you are.
- You feel a great sense of accomplishment by replying quickly to your e-mails and getting that checked off your list.

We're guessing there are many of you out there who can identify with this list. It was easy to write because we've been guilty of all of the above. Both of us have had to work hard to battle this addiction.

Okay, it's confession time: one of us still struggles with it more than the other one does.

Pattye: Scott, would you answer your damn phone? I hate it when you don't have it with you when I want to talk to you. (Sorry—I am still working on that addiction thing.)

Scott: What she doesn't know is that I do have it with me; I just don't always feel like talking to her.

If you want to get to the corner office, though, we have some advice: *break the speed habit.* Don't get caught up in that game. Instead, demonstrate your passion for the business by focusing on the content game. Set a goal of being judged by the content of your communications, not the speed with which you respond. Herein lies the difference between employee and boss.

Much of corporate America's addiction to "instant contact" causes them to spend excessive time responding to e-mails with the fewest letters and the fewest words to what, in many cases, is a meaningless e-mail from the "oce"—obsessed corporate environment.

The good news is that you really have an opportunity to stand out by focusing more on content. Send us a thoughtful and insightful memo at 8:00 A.M., detailing a new idea or outlining something intriguing that a competitor has done, and we're impressed.

Take time to think about your response to an e-mail before you hit reply, and we're impressed. Use "reply all" only when it is absolutely necessary and not just to impress everyone with how late you're up, or how fast you respond, and we'd be so delighted that we could cry! If you actually use complete sentences, punctuation, and capitalization, we'd know you at least care about the professional appearance you're making.

Dumb and Dumber

If you are a leader or an aspiring leader, listen up. We want to share something with you that could become a significant competitive advantage for your company. It's also something that should keep you awake at night (but, please, don't send e-mails or leave voice mails while you're up!).

We believe that our obsession with instant communication is contributing to the dumbing down of corporate America. That's right. Corporate America isn't getting smarter. It is getting dumber. Our addiction to "fast" is dramatically limiting our ability to think and to innovate.

We believe the edges are dulling when it comes to proactive, big idea thinking—two abilities everyone expects the person in the corner office to have.

When you spend all your time responding, you lose the ability to envision and dream about the future. And when you lose your ability to dream, you dull your ability to think, and think big. When was the last time you took time to think? To create an environment void of disruption, technology today requires you to be proactive by exercising your right to activate those seldom-used buttons—the off and silent buttons. Do you know where your buttons are, and have you used them lately?

I Don't Have Time to Think Anymore

It's really ironic when you think about it. Throughout my career, I've been rewarded and even promoted for my ability to solve problems and to think creatively. Now that I'm in charge, I realize the one thing I seem to have lost is the time to read, reflect, and most important, the time to think. It seems I spend half or more of my day responding to e-mails and voice mails—often without even thinking through what I'm saying. And I'm afraid it's not just me—everyone around me is doing much the same thing. But I know that innovation is the key to our survival and the survival of our clients. While innovative ideas do spring from inspired thought, the key is having the time to devote to thought. So, in the midst of any busy day, I find I must make an appointment with myself to guarantee I have thinking time.

—Kathy Leonard, President, Advantage Retail (a consortium of Omnicom-owned retail agencies)

While it's easy to get caught up in instant communications and realize you don't have time to think anymore, as the previous story illustrates, it's also easy to use technology as a shield for not thinking, and, even more important, not *engaging* with your fellow coworkers.

This lack of engagement is also a huge contributor to the dumbing down of corporate America. Great ideas, new inventions, breakthrough thinking, and solutions to problems rarely happen in isolation. That's why we are such strong advocates of having a corporate soul mate.

In today's world, it is not unusual for two executives to spend a 45-minute taxi ride from the airport, each obsessed with their BlackBerry, responding to e-mails that at another time he or she would not even have been copied on in the first place. Their dialogue is limited to the occasional "Huh, listen to this e-mail I got from so and so." This dialogue replaces one of them staring out the window and asking, "Why is it that the new product launch failed?" In the latter scenario, an ideation session is started and, often, a big idea is hatched by the time one of them pays the fare. You may think it sounds like Hollywood, but we believe, and we know from experience, that this is still how many ideas occur. Time together, *uninterrupted,* is what corporate America is losing. And that is the last thing it can afford to lose.

Increasingly, though, we see work associates sending e-mails to the person in the next cubicle or leaving voice mails when they know nobody is there. While this certainly reduces potential confrontations, it also reduces collaboration and the ability to build on ideas and make them bigger and better. There is so much to be gained by walking down the hall and asking a colleague to help you finish an idea or to give you feedback on something you're working on. It builds teamwork, but it also builds stronger ideas. How sad that technology allows us to skip that important step—or that anyone would want to do so. Real leaders thrive on input, constructive criticism, and, as we've pointed out before, being builders. And the fact is collaboration builds. Keep that in mind.

We think someone should invent a cloaking device that prohibits you from sending an e-mail or voice mail to anyone in an office next to you. Then you would be required to talk to him or her.

Case in point: In working on this book, we would frequently call each other and read sections or test outline ideas. It would have been easy to just e-mail content to each other, but it wouldn't have produced the same results. By talking to each other, we were able to challenge ideas, make suggestions, and improve the final product.

Conclusion

The tortoise won the race. The hare was overconfident and quit "thinking and planning." Instead, he spent his time doing mindless activities. The tortoise kept his eye on the prize and kept going forward.

Smart always beats fast. Always. Smart gets you to the corner office and helps you stay there.

Five Questions to Ask Yourself to See if You Have the Instinct of Being Smart

1. Is your BlackBerry set up to wake you in the middle of the night if an e-mail comes in?
2. Would you choose to respond even though your answer is incomplete?
3. Have you copied more people than necessary, just because it is easier to do so?

4. Do you make a conscious decision to express thoughts in fewer words because of the nuances of the BlackBerry?
5. Have you ever turned your BlackBerry or your cell phone off in order to provide you with uninterrupted think time?

The correct answers are no, no, no, no, and yes. If you didn't answer this way, you are letting technology use you. Read on for help.

Five Steps to Develop the Instinct of Being Smart

1. Organize your day so that you set specific time aside at the beginning or end of the day to check and respond to messages. Discipline yourself not to check messages throughout the day.
2. Set aside blocks of uninterrupted time (turn off cell phones and BlackBerries) to think and work on major projects.
3. Instead of sending an e-mail asking questions, try doing it in person or by phone.
4. Vow to never again hit "reply all."
5. Type an instant response to an e-mail if you want, but make a rule to put that e-mail in your draft file for at least six hours. Revisit it after you've had time to think and then hit send.

9 Never Leave the Office without It—A Nutcracker, That Is

Scott: Did you know that people thought we were boring and had no life.

Pattye: Are you kidding?

Scott: I mean, we were always talking late at night, we were traveling together and, of course, we could link anything back to business.

Pattye: Okay, I'm still on the boring thing—what the heck do you mean? I consider myself quite interesting.

Scott: I'm sure you are now, but to be honest, how many times did you divert the conversation or use those you were with as an ad hoc focus group?

Pattye: Hmmm, let me think—I had probably better take the fifth.

Scott: Just as I thought. I can remember calling you from vacations, dinners, ballgames, the theater—all because an idea was triggered from somewhere and I needed to find out if you thought it had legs.

Pattye: Well, I don't know if that makes *us* boring. It may make *you* boring.

Scott: Oh, funny, I thought it was *you* who answered the phone and ended up for the next hour (unscheduled I might add), talking about the pros and cons of the idea. And in doing so, it must have been fascinating for those in the car, or at the dinner table, to listen to us talk.

Pattye: I swear you called me one time from a baseball game because of something someone was eating two rows in front of you.

Scott: That wasn't just any product—I saw it and thought of your snack business, and wondered if it would work at your restaurants.

Pattye: You called and we talked about it for the next 30 minutes. Wow, you are right, we are boring!

Scott: Oh, let's just say *focused.* That seems to have a nicer ring to it.

You do not succeed because you do not know what you want, rather you don't want it intensely enough.

—Frank Crane

If you want something intensely enough, you always will be consumed with finding a way to get it.

—Scott and Pattye

Corner Office Instinct 9

Use the World Outside Your Office as Your Muse

Muse (n.): the inspiration that supposedly visits and suggests things to an artist

A recent Gallup research study of CEOs indicates that "workplace engagement" is a powerful factor in catalyzing "outside-the-box" thinking to improve management and business processes.

Businesses everywhere are in search of the ultimate "muse" to provide their company a steady stream of innovative solutions. Leaders spend a lot of time (and money) in an attempt to get their employees to be innovative—to think outside the box. Unfortunately, against inertia, politics, fear, and corporate bureaucracy, creativity often doesn't stand a chance.

Innovation is happening out there, though. So where do employees get the creativity, drive, and confidence to venture outside of the safe solution and come up with innovative answers? As you have already read, according to Gallup, much of the "push" comes from a person's level of engagement with the workplace.

When you engage with work, you move from working a job to managing a career (see Instinct 7). Once you begin to manage a career, you realize the long-term benefits of taking initiative, and often these initiatives are solution-based. Once you are engaged and managing your own career, you find you don't care where, when, or how you come up with the innovative solution; you only care that you *do* come up with the idea. It is one thing to say you seek innovative solutions; it is quite another to develop the discipline needed to deliver them. It's the difference between any office and the corner office, quite frankly.

We speak from experience when we say that innovation and big ideas don't show up on demand. They aren't slotted in your day timer like a personnel review or a meeting with your boss. Despite the unpredictability of idea generation, there is one thing we know for sure: If you limit the time you are thinking about the business to when you are at work, the corner office is probably not for you. If you are engaged with the workplace, however, chances are quite good you will begin to view everything as your inspiration—your muse, if you will. Then, the sky is the limit.

What the Heck Is a Nutcracker?

The concept of the *nutcracker* is truly quite simple. But don't let the simplicity fool you. It is a powerful tool that separates the best from the rest. At first glance, many would think packing your nutcracker is just another way of saying "take your work home with you." They would be wrong. This is not about those who take their inbox and their busy work home with them. Many people do that. Some of them actually move it from their cars to their houses, where it sits quietly, ignored for an evening of Monday Night Football or completion of your third-grader's science project.

The nutcracker is symbolic of the emotional and intellectual drive to crack the code on any major and pressing business issues. When you pack your nutcracker, you leave the office *with* those issues and, as a result, you have a curiosity and drive that forces you to use the outside world as your muse.

In our case, we always knew what those issues were and our nutcrackers went everywhere with us as a result.

There are many people who seek that next promotion because they believe they are the best of class in their departments. At the end of the day, however, when they press that elevator button, step in, and see that door close, they become the modern-day version of Fred Flintstone. The elevator door closes and you can almost hear them yell out a big "YABBA-DABBA-DOO," which is Bedrock-speak for "I'm outta here." They feel a sense of relief as they pull out of the parking lot and see the office slowly vanish in their rearview mirrors. They may have a bulging briefcase, but they are working on the wrong stuff.

These aren't bad employees who should be banished to low-level positions where they will waste away into oblivion. Unfortunately, though, these are the people who seldom are thought of as leaders, who rarely bring new and unique insights to the table, but who will still complain when they are passed over for a promotion. As we reflect back on our careers, a major contributor to our success was that we *never* left the office without our nutcracker (and a couple of big nuts).

What You Can Learn from an *Oreo*

As a volunteer for the national Arthritis Foundation, I had been asked to make a presentation explaining the concept of branding to the board of trustees. Branding can be a difficult concept to explain, particularly when it involves changing to a new image and one consistent message and look. I hadn't figured out how to make the presentation yet, but my nutcracker was in my pocket. I was at a homeroom party for my daughter and noticed that we had two packages of cookies on the table. One package was "Oreos" and the other was a generic brand—but the same crème-filled chocolate cookie. The "Oreos" were eaten quickly, but the kids left the other cookies. That was it—the concept of branding! So before the presentation, I set out a tray of assorted treats—always with one branded and one generic of the same treat. And I watched and prayed that the board members would behave like the second graders. They did. Those treats became the cornerstone of the presentation; the board approved the branding recommendation as a result. It was a good thing my nutcracker was with me at that homeroom party.

—*Pattye*

It would be nice and tidy if business issues were as simple as day trading stocks; you clear everything out at the end of the day and start all over again the next day. Unfortunately, the corporate reality is that business solutions take time, insight, and creative thinking to solve, or crack, if you will.

We strongly believe that creative problem solving is stronger outside of the workplace. That is one of the reasons management teams have off-site retreats to help solve big problems (and then everyone attends the meetings with their BlackBerries). The belief is that the mind is more open and receptive to new ideas when away from the workplace.

What's in Your Briefcase?

Make it a point to observe your fellow coworkers when they leave the office. Most pack mail and magazines when they leave the office, and they view the end of the day as permission to stop thinking about work. Those who have their sights set on the corner office pack the burning business issues and their nutcracker.

Here are a few examples of what happens when you pack your nutcracker, and how it helps you view the everyday issues from a different angle:

- Rather than singing to a song in a traffic jam, you play "what if" games on how to crack a new market. Or if you do listen to a song, a certain lyric sparks an idea on a new product.
- Rather than racing through the grocery store, you strike up a conversation with an employee in the produce section and it sparks an idea.
- While at dinner, your daughter drops something into her milk, and, at that moment instead of scolding her, you see a potential product merger, and you write it down on a napkin for future reference (this actually happened).
- Rather than roll over and go back to sleep, you get up from bed to draw out a diagram that could be the answer to a logistics problem.

Even a Nutcracker Loves the Great American Pastime

There is little I love more in the summer than to go to the ballpark and watch the local major league baseball team. The sun, the beer, the crack of the bat and—hey, wait a second—what the heck is that person eating three rows in front of me? There, in this giant box, was a gathering of food begging for my attention—a giant helping of tater tots, sour cream, and chili. A quick inventory told me that our client had every one of those products in-store and that, given the battle that was underway for the snack business, this had to be a sign. If I saw it from three rows back, imagine how it would sell full screen on television. To my buddies' lack of surprise, in the third inning I picked up the phone and called Pattye. It was Saturday, but there was nowhere she was going to be that I couldn't interrupt her with this new product newsflash. I left a message; she returned the call around the fifth inning; and for the next two innings, we talked sales and product potential.

Without the nutcracker, I would have still seen this product, but I wouldn't have seen it for what it could mean to our client. Now if I can only remember if we won the game.

—*Scott*

The important thing to understand is that the nutcracker concept is about an emotional and intellectual commitment (a state of mind, if you will) that creates an ongoing restlessness until the solutions are created.

These are just a few examples of what the nutcracker represents:

- The nutcracker has no inbox, no boxes to be checked off, and no reply to sender tabs; rather, it is about ideas and concepts that have little regard for time or place.
- The nutcracker is about having that sense of competitiveness deep inside you that says I want to be the one who cracks this initiative and I want my name attached to the solution.

- The nutcracker represents the individual drive to figure *it* out, whatever *it* is.
- The nutcracker represents the uneasiness and emptiness you feel until the problem is solved.
- The presence or absence of a nutcracker will determine in many ways if you have what it takes to make it to the corner office.

Can I Get Frequent Flyer Miles for My Nutcracker?

Not until we started writing this book did I confess something to my coauthor. I finally admitted to her that she was a marked woman whenever several of us flew together to meetings over the year. No one wanted to sit with her because her passion for the business was downright exhausting. I usually took the "bullet" for the team—or so they thought. The reality is we both had our nutcrackers out and were eager to engage in conversations that might help us crack those big nuts. The conversations may have been about work, about family, about sports, and they may have even involved the passengers sitting by us. But while others were sleeping or reading the latest whodunit, we were cracking nuts. Ironically, we'd be cracking nuts mostly on Southwest Airline flights.

—*Scott*

Our stories also show you the value of having a soul mate. In each case, you notice how we called each other to work through the validity of the idea, discuss initial barriers, and the overall potential of the idea.

The nutcracker theory also works alone. You should begin to apply this theory as early in your career as possible. As it becomes second nature to view things outside the office, not as they appear, but rather as a catalyst for creative problem solving, we promise—when you least expect it—you'll be able to use the nutcracker time and time again to crack that big nut.

Boring Drive + Great Music = Nutcracker

Here is another quick example of finding a solution to a pressing problem. Each year, I spoke to attendees at Sonic's national convention, and I always worked hard to ensure that my presentation had special meaning and captured the heart of our brand. This particular year, though, I was coming up dry. I knew I wanted to talk about the power of love and the value of relationships, but I was uninspired. That nut went everywhere with me, but I was running out of time. One day, I was making a four-hour drive to see my daughter perform at a Summer Arts Institute. It was such a boring drive that I stopped on the way and bought a CD. I'm not a music buff and I didn't even know what to buy, but I saw an Eric Clapton CD so I bought it. This was totally out of character for me—I usually spent the time on my cell phone leaving messages for people, but that day I wanted music. As I'm driving and listening to my new CD, the nutcracker hopped out of my pocket and cracked that big speech nut. One of the songs on the CD was "Let

Your Love Grow," and the title and the lyrics expressed perfectly what I was trying to convey at our convention. I probably listened to that song 20 times and, as I did, my convention presentation just fell into place. I was so excited that I left messages for people telling them I had figured it out. Of course, I called Scott and made him listen to the song through my cell phone so he could tell me if I was crazy. I had cracked another nut!

—*Pattye*

Conclusion

Here's an interesting exercise for you. Think of the ideas or innovations that you're proud of and make a list of where you were and what you were doing when you thought of them. When we took an inventory of our ideas and innovations, we realized that, in almost every case, we were somewhere other than the office—a baseball game, a charity event, a school party, the theater, an airplane, jogging on a treadmill (yes, we met at the hotel gym and jogged side-by-side and dreamed up solutions). Some people who worked with us used to roll their eyes and groan when we started conversations with "We had an idea this morning while we were jogging." Quite frankly, in our view, they didn't have their nutcrackers with them. They didn't make it to the corner office either.

As leaders, we dreamed of the moment when associates marched into our offices and presented thoughtful, imaginative, and (this is the most important part) *unsolicited* business solutions. Right or wrong, the effort showed they had the passion they needed to make a difference, and the passion they needed to move up. It showed they were taking more than magazines home with them.

What are you taking home with you?

Five Questions to Ask Yourself to See if You Have the Instinct of Taking Your Nutcracker with You

1. Is there a notepad next to your bed?
2. Do you draw others in to serve as a sounding board for your solutions?
3. Have you scribbled a note on a napkin while out?
4. Do you leave the office at the office?
5. Is it important to you to be recognized as a creative problem solver?

If you answered yes, yes, yes, no, and yes, then start cracking. Otherwise, see the following five steps.

Five Steps to Develop the Instinct of Taking Your Nutcracker with You

1. At the start of each week, put two outstanding issues on a sticky note and put it on the dashboard of your car. It will serve to redirect your imagination while sitting in traffic.
2. Start some activity that allows your mind to wander—walking, jogging, yoga, sitting in a park—anything that allows you an extended period where your mind has space to fill.
3. Have a "What if Wednesday" where there is one issue you want to solve. Make sure you pursue it all day. Talk to people you encounter during the day about this issue and

make sure it stays top-of-mind. We promise you'll hear new thinking if you listen.

4. Occasionally, find time to challenge a myth, the status quo, or what is considered a business truth in your company. Come up with all the reasons to challenge this "truth" and find ways to test it. You may still end up supporting the status quo, but the practice is great for breakthrough thinking and objective analysis. Most product breakthroughs come from a challenge to conventional wisdom or the status quo.
5. Read business books on creative thinking. Read things outside your area. Do interesting and different things.

10 Speak Now or Forever Hold Your Peace and Possibly Your Career

Scott: So, when did you figure out how important it was to be a superb communicator?

Pattye: Now, don't laugh—but I learned it watching *Bewitched* when I was eight.

Scott: You go, Samantha.

Pattye: Samantha? No way. I was fascinated by the advertising world and both Darren Stevens and Larry Tate. In fact, I used to play "advertising." I'd line up my Barbie dolls and present campaigns to them.

Scott: Pattye—how do I say this? Well, here it goes—that's not normal. While the rest of us were playing with marbles, you were making presentations to your Barbie dolls? Oh, my . . .

Pattye: I even remember some of the presentations—don't tell me you don't remember any presentations you made up or took part in as a kid?

Scott: Yes, but for different reasons, which apparently I now have to share. When I was eight, I was in a program sitting on stage in front of a lot of people. And I was scared, very scared—so scared that I peed in my pants, in fact. Happy now?

Pattye: Well, you're a powerful presenter now, so you obviously learned: (1) to go to the restroom first and (2) how to get over stage fright.

Scott: Actually, what I learned was this: If you're going to pee in your pants, make sure you are wearing dark slacks, and don't sit in those plastic chairs with holes in them.

They may forget what you said, but they will never forget how you made them feel.

—Carl W. Buechner

If you can't move your audience, then move over.

—Scott and Pattye

Corner Office Instinct 10

Find Your Voice and Never Take It for Granted

Voice (n.): a medium of communication; the right to express an opinion

A February 2001 Gallup poll found that 40 percent of adults have a fear of public speaking.

Most of us weren't born as gifted orators, and we trust that most of you didn't spend your childhood making speeches to your dolls. Yet, it seems as though many people resign themselves to being average public speakers and are willing to live with the dread (and the nausea) that comes with the walk to the podium, or even to the front of the room. We find it ironic that accomplished professionals will invest significant time and energy in self-improvement, in learning a new language—in just about any skill, except public speaking.

While a full range of skills and expertise is necessary to make it to the corner office, there is probably no skill that benefits you more than the ability to persuade, motivate, and inspire others with your words.

That's why finding your voice is critically important. What do we mean by that? Quite simply, finding your voice is about figuring out what your most effective communications style is. The good news is there isn't just one style that works. Effective communicators can be soft-spoken, passionate, funny, or energetic, but they do have one thing in common—they learn early on what works for them, and they spend the rest of their lives studying, practicing, and improving. Never taking your voice for granted means that you should never underestimate how important this skill is, and you should never stop working to improve it.

There is nothing more rippling and potentially destructive to an organization than having someone in a leadership position who is consistently second-guessed. We are willing to bet that a large number of the second guessers are those who were not moved to follow the leader's vision in the first place. They may not have been moved because the leader in question had poor communication skills and was incapable of connecting his (or her) vision to the beliefs and desires of those responsible for making it happen.

In corporate America, most associates long to be led. They long to march behind a leader who has a vision and articulates it in such a way that the destination is believed to be reachable, and that good things will come to all when they arrive. The passion and support of those who follow is almost infectious. It is as if they have been moved to take part in a bigger cause beyond the mundane day-to-day nature of their work.

Are You Willing to Take Voice Lessons?

Myth: Most people believe that they are not good public speakers and will never be.

Fact: You absolutely can improve your speaking skills and overcome your fear.

To underscore how important this is to advancing your career, we both can share examples of people being passed over for promotions because they were lacking this skill. To move up, you have to be able to inspire confidence in those above and below you, and that requires being a good communicator. It's heartbreaking to have to pass over well-qualified employees because they can't verbally express themselves well, and they haven't been willing to invest in improving this skill.

Invest is the key word. We know that you can become a better communicator if you invest the time to become better. We also know that you will not dramatically improve your communication skills unless you do make the investment. What exactly are we talking about? Here are some simple ways you can invest in becoming a better presenter:

- Join an organization like Toastmasters whose sole purpose is to help you become a better speaker.
- Be a student of great speakers. Watch political conventions and take notes on the techniques and the approaches the various politicians use. You will see some of the world's most powerful speakers at these conventions. But don't stop there: Pay attention to every speaker you hear, from your preacher to the president of your company. How did they present? What did they do that was good and what did they do that didn't work? Keep a notebook with these thoughts and ideas, and with stories and quotations that you can use in the future.
- Volunteer for civic organizations and be willing to chair task forces or committees where you are required to give reports. The more often you do this, the more comfortable you will be with it.

- Ask your friends, colleagues, or boss to provide you with constructive criticism whenever you do make a report or give a presentation.
- Invest in seminars, books, and tapes on how to improve your speaking (and writing) skills. If you're going to be a good speaker, you also have to write a good speech.

Note to parents: While it is never too late to improve your communications skills, it is also never too early to start working on them. Make sure your children understand early on that this is an important skill for them to learn. Schools spend very little time on this. Typically, students present book reports, but there is no time spent on how to do it. Encourage your students to join the debate team and to take speech communications classes in college (in our opinion, this should be required in high school and college). Persuade your children to attend seminars and presentations with you, and talk about the speeches and the presenters. Help them practice. Most important, don't transfer to them a fear of public speaking. Show them that this is a skill just like riding a bike. You're going to have some pain at first, but once you get comfortable with it, it will be enjoyable, and it will be a means of transportation (translation—it will help you get where you want to go in your career).

How Do You Get to Carnegie Hall?

We're sure you've heard this joke. "How do you get to Carnegie Hall?" "Practice, practice, practice." Well, practicing is also the way to the corner office.

The great news is that the more you practice and rehearse public speaking, the better you will become. It's almost guaranteed. So much of improving is related to gaining a level of confidence and comfort with speaking. When anxiety is the major barrier to exceptional performance, familiarity will breed comfort, and from comfort will come an improved performance.

We know that the idea of practicing or (heaven forbid) getting help for public speaking throws most of us into a rather elevated state of denial. To get to the corner office, though, you must elevate your level of self-awareness and admit you need and want to improve. This level of self-awareness is hard to acquire if you have been on the corporate fast-track route, and most of your time has been spent having your back patted by others telling you what a good job you have been doing. It's easy to convince yourself that your skills are fine—you're just as good as others—so there is no need to spend time on this.

We have two responses to this: First, "just as good" doesn't get you to the corner office. Second, you're not as good as you think you are. This is a skill that requires constant attention for even the most accomplished orators.

For Ladies Only

I was fortunate early in my career to be in a position to observe lots of senior management presentations—to bankers, analysts, and employees. Okay, to be more specific, the exact position I was in was sitting next to the slide projector with the remote control in my hands and a copy of the speech in my lap. It was amazing what I learned from that vantage point. This is not meant to be sexist, but one of the things that I observed is that men were often cut more slack for their poor communications skills. If a male executive was a poor speaker, the conclusion would often be that he wasn't a very skilled speaker, but it didn't translate to his skills as a leader. I observed just the opposite effect with female speakers. If a woman made a bad presentation, the conclusion was often that she wasn't very good at her job, or a competent leader. For me, the decision was simple. As a woman, if I wanted to succeed, I would have to become an excellent communicator. I worked hard at it, and I absolutely believe my communications skills got me noticed and promoted.

Ladies, like it or not, life isn't fair. Trust me—an ability to communicate will help even the playing field. The reality is, excellent speaking skills will help you get ahead whether you're a man or a woman, but they are essential if you're a woman.

—*Pattye*

Whether you are a woman or a man, being a superb communicator can play a big role in your future success. To help you with your investment in this instinct, we've outlined five tips for becoming a better communicator.

Tip 1: It All Starts with Good Material

Jay Leno may be a great comedian, but he is only as good as his material. He has mastered the delivery, but that wouldn't matter if his material was bad. The same holds true for you.

The first place to start is with your presentation, speech, or report. Take time to research unique facts, insights, and findings. This will make your presentation more persuasive as well as more believable. That is how you get good material.

Go to the Library

I can't tell you how many times I've gone to the library or bookstore to find facts and inspiration for my speeches. One time in particular stands out. I was going to be giving a presentation in Hawaii, so I checked out several books on Hawaiian culture, customs, and history. I discovered that the Hawaiian word *Ohana* means extended family. Because my audience viewed themselves as a "family," I was able to weave that word and other examples of Hawaiian customs into my speech—including a funny story about a powerful Hawaiian goddess.

—*Pattye*

Tip 2: Say It Out Loud

To the novice, this section is going to sound somewhat elementary; however, the lesson is monumental. Great athletes and great actors practice and rehearse as if their performance was real—you need to do the same. Once you've developed your material, you need to put it to the test. Read it out loud. Does it sound right? How long is it? No matter what your answer is, we can tell you it's likely to be too long. Go back and edit it more tightly. And every edit requires you to read it over and over—out loud.

Tip 3: How Much Should You Practice?

Practice more than you think you need to. As you get more polished and comfortable as a speaker, you can probably get away with practicing less. *Note:* We didn't say as you attain higher executive positions, you can practice less. You may be the CEO of a major corporation, but, if you're not polished, you still need to prepare and practice because all eyes are on you.

It's Okay to Have Rituals

As we started working on this chapter, we discovered that we both have rituals that we use to help us get ready for big presentations. What was surprising was how similar they are.

I'm totally obsessive about practicing any speech I give. It doesn't matter how often I've spoken in public, or what size group I'm speaking to, I guarantee you I will practice my presentation. If I'm giving off-the-cuff remarks, I'll still run through them out loud in front of my bathroom mirror.

In fact, my bathroom mirror is my worst critic. If I'm giving a prepared speech (even if I have a teleprompter), I will practice it a dozen times in front of the mirror. But that's not enough. I'm usually in a hotel the night before a big speech, and that's good because this ritual really works better alone. When I get into bed, the last thing I do before I turn out the lights is I read my speech out loud—lying flat on my back in bed. Then, the next morning, the first thing I do when the alarm goes off is read the speech out loud again—before I get up. That's become a good luck ritual for me.

—*Pattye*

She forgot to mention that her Barbie dolls are lined up on the bathroom counter, nodding and clapping enthusiastically. I also practice my presentations out loud a number of times, but I prefer the comfort of my living room (must be a guy thing). I do have a similar nighttime ritual, though. I always sleep with a copy of my speech under my pillow. It's my good luck charm as well. And quite frankly, it requires less work and allows for more sleep than Ms. Moore's approach (another guy thing).

—*Scott*

Tip 4: Don't Practice Bad Habits

If you mumble your words, shift from foot to foot, or say "uh" every other word, begin to break the habit. If you have bad habits and just keep practicing them, chances are you are going to make it difficult to improve.

That's where constructive criticism comes in. You have to ask your boss or your friends how your presentation was, and you have to get straight answers. Don't ask, "Was my presentation good?" It's hard to answer that. Instead ask, "Do you have any suggestions on what I could do to improve my presentation skills?"

We can't tell you how many times we have called each other to review presentations. We have sent written copies to each other to critique, and then we have practiced in front of each other—sometimes over the phone and sometimes in person. We made sure we got confirmation and critiques.

Make sure you listen to all criticism—from people you respect, and even from perfect strangers. In all criticism, there is at least one grain of truth.

Once you get that feedback, make the changes, and then practice the new habits. Practice in front of a mirror, in front of someone, in front of your fridge, but please, please practice!

Take All Feedback

I attended the convention of a franchisee many years ago. There had to be nearly 300 people in attendance. At some part of the convention, they gave each individual three things they should attempt to work on. With over 300 attendees, how specific could these suggestions be? I figured they would be as vague as the daily horoscope and about as useful. I was wrong. In my case, one of the items I was told I needed to work on was improving eye contact during presentations. It was hard to listen to and accept this criticism, but, to this day, I thank that man—Jack Hartnett—for caring enough about me to tell me. And I worked on it, from that day forward.

—*Scott*

Tip 5: Find Ways to Connect with Your Audience on a Personal Level

Connecting with your audience on a personal level is absolutely critical. In order to connect with your audience, you have to take the time to learn something about them. Do some homework. Show the audience that you are glad to be there. Show them that you have done them the courtesy of preparation—not only practicing but also learning something about the audience.

Once you've done your homework and practiced, here are several different ways to help achieve that personal connection:

- *Appropriate use of humor:* Audiences like to see that you have a sense of a humor and they like to laugh (as long as it is not mean-spirited). If you're not a funny person, then use humor sparingly. One of us is basically a stand-up comic (that would be Scott) and one of us isn't all that funny (that would be Pattye). We wouldn't be using our own "voice" if we suddenly switched places. Make sure you know your own limitations.
- *Stage presence:* Be willing to step away from the podium, and walk the stage or the room. Take a microphone out into the audience and ask questions, or ask for feedback. The self-confidence you portray by walking around, sitting on a stool, or strolling through the audience is contagious. People will become more relaxed, they will relate better to what you're saying, and they will assume that your confidence as a speaker translates to your skills as a leader. (And they are right—it does.)
- *Willingness to make fun of yourself:* Many people have trouble with this and we believe it's because they get caught up in their own self-importance or what they perceive to be acceptable demeanor for an executive or an up-and-coming executive. We say hogwash! People want to relate to their leaders. They want to know leaders are human, and that they are willing to have fun, to appear silly, and (gasp!) to wear costumes. If you believe it demeans you or your position, then we think you have too little confidence to be in that position anyway, so move over.

Shoot-Out at the OK Corral

I had the opportunity to observe the correct way to eliminate barriers and connect with an audience when I watched the new chairman and CEO of our company speak at our annual conference. This distinguished gentleman had been on our company's board and was tapped to step in as chairman and CEO after the abrupt departure of a longtime chief. This was his first chance to meet the attendees and their first chance to check him out as well.

The conference had a Western theme. You might have expected this leader to come out on stage in a business suit and maybe wear a cowboy hat. Well, he didn't do that. Instead, he came in from the back of the room in a leather duster, boots, a cowboy hat, a fake mustache, and a six-shooter. Before he got on stage, he had a shoot-out with staff members dressed as competitors! Then, he got on stage and addressed the group with a mustache that wouldn't stay on.

Not a very CEO-like thing to do, but it was a brilliant move that spoke volumes about this leader's understanding of the situation and his role. With that action, he broke down many emotional barriers, signaled that he understood our company's culture, and conveyed the message that things were going to be okay. Keep in mind that he started his career as a CPA—just in case you were thinking only marketing types do stuff like this. Actually, *leaders* do stuff like this!

—Kim McBee, Vice President, Marketing,
Red Robin Gourmet Burgers

Conclusion

Consider if you will what we believe are the three biggest reasons why potential corporate fast trackers do not get better at public speaking:

1. They ignore it.
2. They tell themselves they are not as bad as they really are.
3. They devalue the role it plays in getting promoted.

We hope you don't fall into any of these three categories because being a great communicator really moves you onto the express elevator to the top. There's an added benefit as well. When you find your public speaking voice, you will discover that you are also more comfortable articulating your position in meetings, taking a stand for something you believe in with senior management and even in convincing your spouse to buy that new house. The benefits are too numerous to mention, but they all add up to leadership.

Okay, stop reading now! Come listen to us speak. Take notes on what to do and what not to do. And, by all means, critique us. We want and need your feedback so we can get better.

Five Questions to Ask Yourself to See if You Have the Instinct of Finding Your Voice

1. Are you willing and able to admit to yourself and others that a big part of your job (no matter what you do) is dependent on your ability to communicate effectively?
2. Do you seek brutally honest criticism in an effort to become a better communicator?
3. Do you pay close attention to other speakers and make notes during presentations?

4. Have you ever practiced your presentation in front of your spouse, a friend, or a work soul mate?
5. Are you willing to put on a costume or act silly in front of other people?

If you answered yes to all of the above, then you are indeed on the way to finding your voice.

Five Steps to Develop the Instinct of Finding Your Voice

1. Ask someone to listen and critique as you rehearse your presentations—and tell him or her that you want total honesty.
2. Enroll (on your own) in a public speaking class or seminar in your area.
3. Take an introduction-to-acting class at the local community college. This will begin to break down some walls in regard to performance.
4. Treat every audience as if they were brand new. **Important:** Stop the habit of less preparation for those you are familiar with.
5. Commit to learning one thing from every speaker you hear. Have a little book with you. It can be something you would like to incorporate, or even something you want to make sure you *never* do.

11 Working the Room Is Not Just for Politicians

Scott: You know, this instinct came very naturally for both of us, don't you think?

Pattye: Without a doubt. I never really liked sitting in my office. No matter what stage of my career, I enjoyed getting out and talking to customers or employees.

Scott: That, Ms. Moore, is an understatement. I think our teams expected us to spend less and less time in the field as we moved up, but it didn't happen.

Pattye: True. I got the most amazing looks when, as president, I attended a co-op meeting in a small market. Our employees out in the field looked at me as if to say, "Why did you take the time to fly out here for this meeting?"

Scott: I got the same thing, and my answer was always that there is something to learn regardless of the size of the meeting. But what continued to amaze and sometimes annoy me was how much you loved the concept of a good old-fashioned road trip.

PATTYE: Ah, those road trip days. My favorite time was when a group of us ate our way across Alabama, evaluating new menus, and developing marketing plans for down stores.

SCOTT: Maybe we were too accessible. Maybe we should have just asked for it to be done and not actually driven the markets with our teams.

PATTYE: Look me in the eye. Do you really believe that?

SCOTT: No, but it sounded politically correct to say.

PATTYE: But we learned so much, although I do think you could have eaten less on that trip across Alabama. Didn't you go to your hotel room and get sick?

SCOTT: Yes, Pattye, I did. Once again, your photographic memory has been used for evil rather than good. You don't need to inform everyone that I got sick.

PATTYE: Sorry, but you sure looked green the next morning.

SCOTT: Enough.

To lead people, walk beside them.

—Lao-Tsu, Chinese Philosopher

People more passionately follow personalities and character than they do positions.

—Scott and Pattye

Corner Office Instinct 11

Be Seen, Be Heard, and Be Approachable

Approachable (adj.): easy to meet or deal with, friendly

The Executive Bench Survey™ by executive consulting firm RHR International looked at the characteristics companies seek in their future leadership. Most respondents cited the ability to build strong relationships internally and externally (86 percent), followed by openness to change and growth (81 percent).

The ability to build relationships is a critical leadership skill set. Unfortunately, it's not one that gets much attention. We know it is highly unusual, given the current state of affairs, to point to politicians as a credible and respected form of "best practice," but the fact is politicians always have and always will know how to "work a room." While the outcome of their glad-handing sprint through a ballroom may create a false sense of concern and accessibility, there is something to learn from the power of having a personal conversation, regardless of how brief. The power of being seen, being heard, and engaging in one-on-one conversation is conveniently overlooked by most executives (especially if the dialogue is with someone down, and not up, on the corporate ladder) because it is time consuming. Quite honestly, many view it as a waste of time as well.

But why are we seeing, more and more, the emergence of "town hall" meetings as a marketing ploy for politicians? Because they are effective. These made-for-television events are designed to show that the politician is in touch with the "average Joe." While the format may be political smoke and mirrors, the idea is a valid one for corporate leaders. A connection to your constituency is crucial in creating the kind of passionate followers any effective and strong leader needs.

Patio Music

I'll admit it took some courage to ask the president of Sonic if she wanted to hear the song I had just written about the company. I had heard Ms. Moore was visiting Sonics in Nashville, Tennessee, so I made the two-hour drive from the drive-in I managed just to see her. I had met her the year before at a crew competition and had told her I was writing a song about Sonic. She said she couldn't wait to hear it, but as I approached her that afternoon to ask if she remembered me and the song, I started to think how naive I was.

She had probably met hundreds of Sonic employees during the past year—she wasn't going to remember a 20-year-old aspiring musician. Besides that, she was probably just being polite when she said she couldn't wait to hear it. But I'd driven a long way, so I got up the courage and asked her if she wanted to hear the song. To my surprise, she smiled at me and said she would "love" to hear it. I think I shocked her when I ran to my car, got my guitar, and came back to sit with her. I will never forget that day the rest of my life. There I was, playing my guitar and singing on the patio of a Sonic and my audience was the president of a major fast-food chain. She listened, smiled, and most important, she was genuine in her appreciation for what I had performed. So much so, in fact, that she asked me to play in front of 3,000 people at the company's national convention (my largest audience at that point). When somebody that high up takes the time to listen and engage with people, regardless of their title—well, to me, that is the true definition of a real leader. I guess she knew what she was doing because my dream has just come true and my band, Trailer Choir, will be opening for Toby Keith's summer 2007 concert tour. Thank you, Ms. Moore, for taking the time to listen. I would guess that there are few in your position who would.

—*Vencent Hickerson*

Take This Door and Shove It

The Biggest Obstacle to Being Approachable

We want you to think about something: a door. That's right, a door. The simple four-letter word that defines a partition between your office and the rest of the company is, in our view, the culprit in what we call the "cocooning of corporate executives." This eight-foot by three-foot piece of wood has a symbolism and a power seldom seen elsewhere in corporate America.

This simple office feature has the ability to (1) limit executives from walking the office, (2) allow someone to define his or her worth in the company, and (3) cause many to waste valuable energy and emotion speculating about the events being conducted on the other side of the door.

While this instinct focuses primarily on the first result, allow us a diversion to briefly address the final two results.

Can people really allow a door to define their corporate worth? You bet they can. We have both worked in environments where having a door was some ridiculous symbolic level of achievement. We have fielded more than our share of complaints when an associate came in and complained, "I've been here longer and Roger now has an office with a door." We have spent hours discussing new office space, and how many offices with doors we could accommodate. For some reason, somewhere it has been instilled in people that a door on your office means you have *arrived.*

Talk about a crock.

What does having a door really mean? It means the associate now has the ability to close a door and shut the entire company out—and to send a message to stay out. It means you can now have phone conversations in total privacy. It also means you can conduct a lot of inappropriate business in your office because you have a door.

And do people really pay attention to who it is behind those closed doors? You bet they do. Put the right combination of individuals in an office, close the door, and you might as well close the office. The speculation will run rampant until the door opens because it "must be serious if they closed the door."

We know you are thinking that there are confidential things that need to be discussed, and the door must be closed for that. That's true, so meet in a conference room. A closed conference room door says, "We're having a meeting." A closed office door says, "Someone is getting fired," or "There is a plot to take over the company being hatched," or (let's cut to the chase) "They're talking about me."

However, having a door doesn't say, "Hey, follow me; I'm a great leader."

Let's go back to the first point we made about a door limiting a person's ability to walk the office. There is an interesting phenomenon that we have witnessed firsthand. It seems that the higher you move up the corporate ladder, the more the door provides an entry into the ever-expanding square footage that mirrors your most recent promotion. Too often the office (and the door) is viewed as the prize—the payoff for years and years of hard work. Finally, you have a view, a window, and two chairs, and, gosh-darn it, you are going to soak it in.

Why Do His Plants Keep Dying?

Early in my career, I worked for a man who never emerged from his office. He didn't have a door—we all had cubicles—but he did have a corner cubicle that was bigger, and it had a view and two chairs. He also had it arranged in a way that was as closed off as you could get it. He strategically placed some large plants near the cubicle opening to create a screen of sorts. He went into his office in the morning and never came out. We used to speculate that he must pee on his plants, and that was why they kept dying. He never came to my office. He never walked the halls. Occasionally I was called to his office, and it made me very nervous. To this day, I don't really have a clue what he did all day. Here's the irony: we worked in the communications department.

—*Pattye*

We have all worked for those individuals who view the office as a testament to their struggle and treat it as a squatter would a piece of unclaimed lakeside property. Herein lies the rub. They should be viewing their offices as a launch pad at NASA from which they go out to explore and better understand their universe, or as the base from which the politician connects with his constituency.

Size Does Not Matter

When you walk the halls of your company, and are seen and heard by those you work with, you become that much more approachable. But you have to get up, get out of your office, and walk.

This cocooning of executives is best demonstrated by some out-of-date law that states that he who has the bigger office doesn't have to move. Too many leaders operate under the guise of "if someone wants to meet with me, we'll meet in my office because I'm senior in title, and my office is bigger." While most won't admit it, this practice exists in virtually every office in the country. Yet, when you put it down in writing, it appears to have its roots in some elementary school experience with a sandbox.

We would like to see where it is stated that *he who has the bigger office will have all meetings come to him, or that as a person moves up the corporate ladder, the need diminishes to go out and walk the office floors.*

Cocooning is okay at home with your family, big screen television, and surround sound. It's not okay at the office. An executive who is cocooning will become less and less visible, and less and less effective. To put it another way, do you think a politician who engages less and less with those he represents is as likely to be reelected?

If you are a vice president and you have a meeting with a couple of entry-level associates, go meet in their office space. Guess what? On the way to or from this meeting, you will talk to people, and see and hear things that will make you a more effective leader. We guarantee it.

For the record, the more a person moves up within an organization, the more he needs to go out and walk the office floors. With every promotion, you become one more step removed from the majority of the workforce. That simply means you have to work harder to stay in touch.

The person who has a tendency to hunker down in her office obviously believes there is little value in connecting with her constituents and often believes that title alone is all that is needed to become a good leader.

So You All Want a Door, Do You?

We were experiencing record growth and, as a result, were forced to find new office space. Well, everyone had an opinion on what it should be, and the political turf battles were a part of the process. As the configurations went through revision after revision, I don't recall how we got there, but the big idea came. We would alleviate all the whining about who did, and who did not, get an office with a door by making one change to the plan. No one would have a door. No one could walk into the chairman's office or the president's office and complain about not having a door if the top two didn't have one either. Too often senior management operates by a different set of rules than the others. That was not the message we were going to send at our shop.

—Scott

You Work for Them—Not the Other Way Around

There is a fundamental question at play: "What kind of leader do you want to be?" During your career, you will work for a variety of bosses, and you will develop your own style, pulling both good and bad habits from those you've been exposed to. We hope you pull more good than bad, but that will be based on your own self-awareness.

At an early stage, we both realized we were the type who (for better or worse) didn't view our role as the head of the team, but rather as a member of the team who happened to have responsibility for the efforts of the team. Often as we were moving up the corporate ladder, if there was a meeting and the junior people were staying around and putting the presentation materials together, we found it hard to walk out without helping. We don't say this to lay the groundwork for a future Nobel Peace Prize, but to demonstrate that you don't need to change who you are, and what you are, as you move up the ladder. Never forget what it was like to be a new, entry-level, full-of-hope, starry-eyed associate, and how you felt when a member of management stopped by to talk or to help you.

As you move up, you must fight the urge to view your ever-improving office as a destination unto itself. It is important to understand that the office you now occupy is a reflection of your potential, rather than some monument to your past performance. Your potential will be realized in a much grander fashion if you can be the kind of leader who inspires others. To do that, we ask that you revisit the quotation at the start of this chapter: "To lead people, walk beside them."

If that didn't make our point, then consider these words from the most famous general ever, George S. Patton, who stated, "No good decision was ever made in a swivel chair."

Yes, the view from your office may be nicer, your office may have a sofa in it, maybe even a big door—but it is not your home. Instead, look at it as the launching pad from which you operate.

Move Away from That Desk

Get out from behind the desk. You might be amazed at what you see and hear. More important, you will begin to be the kind of leader who will be respected by all. To help you move away from the desk, we would like to offer the following suggestions to get you in front of those you serve and those you depend on to follow:

- When you go for coffee, walk to a different floor to get it.
- Have at least one meeting a day in someone else's office.
- Get off the elevator on a different floor and walk that floor on your way to your office in the morning. Walk a new floor on your way out of the office.
- Eat lunch at least once a week in your employee break or lunch area.
- Have an annual calendar of each employee's anniversary date with the company. Make it a point to stop by their office, or call them, if need be, to offer a "happy anniversary" wish.

No Comfy Owner's Suite for This Owner/CEO

I was fortunate enough to work on the Houston Astros account at the time the current owner Drayton McLane purchased the team. He was a breath of fresh air and, as a result, I have followed the Astros even though I have moved on in my career. I heard a story, and have since found it to be true, that shows the value McLane places on the observations and insights of his customers. Rather than watch the game from some isolated suite, McLane sits in the ballpark, and in the 7th or 8th inning, he walks around the concourse, listening and writing down suggestions from the paying fans.

This is a man who doesn't see his place as removed from his customer. Rather, this is a man who sees his role as one who must continually work to understand what is on the mind of his constituents.

—*Scott*

Conclusion

Take a page from the politicians and actively meet and listen to those who ultimately control your future. Don't just worry about face time with the next rung up the corporate ladder, but realize that the key to your future is the work you will be able to inspire in those who work for you. Be seen, be heard, and be approachable, and you will have a staff that will walk on fire for you. Ultimately, that is what makes a great leader.

Five Questions to Ask Yourself to See if You Have the Instinct to Be Seen, Be Heard, and Be Approachable

1. In the past two weeks, have you spent any one-on-one time with an employee you did not previously know?
2. Do you see people but not know their names and, as a result, say hello but don't ask them their names?
3. Do you have your door closed at least an average of two times a day?
4. Do you ever hold a meeting in the office of someone below you on the corporate ladder?
5. Have you helped those who report to you complete any task, regardless of how insignificant?

If you answered yes, no, no, yes, and yes, congratulations! Your head, heart, and the rest of your body are in the right place as it relates to being an approachable leader.

Five Steps to Develop the Instinct to Be Seen, Be Heard, and Be Approachable

1. Stroll a different floor every day for a month. Take a little note pad and jot down issues or opportunities some employees may share with you.
2. Have lunch with the newest employee once a week.
3. At least one day a week, have as many meetings as possible take place outside of your office.
4. When you come across employees who you do not know, ask them for their names, and introduce yourself.
5. At least once a month (more often would be better), get out in the field and meet with customers and field employees.

12

Sometimes You Have to Face the Firing Squad—Sometimes You *Are* the Firing Squad

Scott: You know the worst part of my job?

Pattye: Oh, this should be good. Let's see, was it that you had to get up early in the morning to get into the office after a night of libations with a client?

Scott: Hardly, I had that part down to a science. No, it was when it came to firing people.

Pattye: Yup, not up there on my top-ten list of things to accomplish at the office. My challenge was that I knew right away if people were going to work out, but, more often than not, I gave them an extended period of time to eventually prove what my gut told me.

Scott: I know what you mean. On my end, since the company also provided my social circle, there were many times when the people I terminated were also friends of mine, and I can't tell you how much that made my day.

Pattye: Maybe it's not so bad that we never got good at that or were quick with the dismissal. But, heck, terminating an employee here or there—that was kids' stuff compared to what I had to do before we began working with each other.

Scott: What did you do, take out an entire department?

Pattye: Worse, I had to fire an entire advertising agency, at a time when we were their largest client, and, without us, they would fold. Oh, and to make it even more suitable for daytime television—I had worked there just a few short years before that.

Scott: Ouch.

Pattye: Sometimes when I think about how I felt that night, I don't angst quite as much when I have to terminate a single employee.

Scott: I guess not. So, is that why the hatchet is in the corner of your office?

Pattye: There is no such thing.

Scott: I know; I just find this topic so damn depressing that I tried to inject some humor.

One of the great talents of all is the talent to recognize and to develop talent in others.

—Frank Tyger

It is also a talent to be able to recognize when those you employ don't *have the talent.*

—Scott and Pattye

Corner Office Instinct 12

Always Remain Objective When Evaluating Talent

Objective (adj.): free of any bias or prejudice caused by personal feelings

Statistics show that firing is particularly tough on the terminator. A 1998 study conducted at 45 hospitals across the United States indicated that managers double their risk of heart attacks during the week after they give someone the ax.

While we found the results of this study more than a little bit alarming, it still is no reason to put off the inevitable if and when the time comes. This is part of leadership; you don't have to enjoy it—but we do want you to live through it. One critical trait that leaders must possess is the ability to objectively assess talent, to make the right hires, and to cut their losses efficiently. It is difficult for a president to overcome a horribly miscast cabinet, as they bumble on issue after issue. It is the president who is deemed ineffective. As the general manager of a ball team, if your draft picks continually underperform, your ability to assess talent is brought into question, as much as your ability to effectively run a major league team.

In the case of corporate America, if you know that you have not made the right hire, you have to cut your losses, and cut them fast. One wild card that is thrown into the mix is when the underperformer is a friend of yours. It happens every day, and it will, at some point, happen to you if you continue to move up the corporate ladder.

When you develop this instinct, you will have the ability to act without guilt, and to place the best interests of your staff and business as your top priority. This instinct directs you to ask yourself: "What is in the best interest of the company?" and to use that as your moral and ethical compass to make objective staffing decisions.

We are not going to sugarcoat it—this may be the most difficult and uncomfortable of the instincts to put into practice. No one enjoys informing someone that his or her career and time with the company has come to an end. No one enjoys sending a father or mother home to inform his or her family that he or she no longer has a job. We are not here to tell you that we got it right every time, but we have learned that there is no way to avoid putting this instinct into practice.

On your way to the corner office, you will be faced with terminating talented individuals. Sometimes, you'll get to call them layoffs, but the impact on the individual is the same: *no job.* That will be gut-check time for you because it will hurt. Even though it hurts, you still need to do what is right for the company. If you lose clients or business gets soft, staff needs to be reduced, and good people with a good work ethic will be let go. And you will be the one to do it.

These are the days you will never forget—as much as you would like to. These are the days that the tears shed in your office may belong to the individual you are firing, but when the day is done and you are alone, the tears are yours.

We hope that you will have very few of these days, but no matter how few of these days you have, they will be too many. These days will also test your mettle as to how much you want to keep expanding your management responsibilities.

When Braniff No Longer Flew

I learned the lesson we just spoke of in my third job. I went to work for the Bloom Agency in Dallas on the Braniff Airlines account. Our goal was to keep Braniff flying, to create enough ticket sales to have the cash to buy the fuel. It was exhilarating, to be quite honest. It was survival marketing. It wasn't about selling a new and improved detergent; it was about helping people keep their jobs. Well, eventually, the airline stopped flying. The brand was no longer. I was called into the president's office and informed that I was going to be let go—that it was not about performance but numbers. The revenue from the airline was gone, and there were many people assigned to the business.

While I worked there about a year, I remember the president asking me if I had any regrets about coming down and taking the job. I said, "Not at all." It was the equivalent of asking a player to pinch hit in game 7 of the World Series with his team down 10 runs. The outcome is inevitable; however, the opportunity to get to the plate in a World Series game is a dream. I thanked him for allowing me to step up to the plate and experience what it was like to try to save an airline. I then went home and started all over again.

—Scott

Fire Mistakes Fast, but Let People Go Gently

As we have said, no one enjoys firing people, or if they do, there are probably some other issues from their childhood that they need to resolve. Most of you will come up with reason after reason to put it off, but, in most cases, even though you have put it off, the person still gets fired. In the meantime, others around the person (who have probably been picking up the slack) will be more and more frustrated that firing her took so long. Then, after the underperformer has been "let go," you will sit there wondering why you didn't do it sooner, because you knew a long time ago she was not going to work out.

There is an old saying that it isn't the people you fire who will make your life miserable, it is the people you don't.

We understand it is human nature to avoid the undesirable. However, here are six tips to challenge the way you think about terminating an individual that may help you begin to develop a keen sense of objectivity:

1. *Think of the impact on the other associates and on the team as a whole.* If you look at it from that perspective, you may find it easier to "pull the plug," if you will. Those employees who you respect and admire are often the ones most closely affected by an ill-matched employee.
2. *Remember that termination is not always about poor performance.* Often, it is a case of mismatched skills, poor timing, poor hiring, or just straight financials. Don't necessarily approach firing someone as a permanent indictment that the individual is flawed and a failure—or that you are the one making the indictment. Sometimes the failure is yours, not his or hers. In other cases, it is not a good match. Chances are, if you know it's not a good match, the individual knows it, and you may actually be doing him or her a favor. *Here's a word to the wise, however:* Don't tell the person that you're doing them a favor by firing him or her, and don't expect that person to think that way for years.

3. *Deliver the message to the person in a caring, respectful way.* If there are performance issues, then share those with the individual in a gentle way so that he or she can learn and move on. You owe it to the employee to level with her about why she is being fired. Too many times, we've seen leaders not want to hurt someone's feelings or confront an issue, so they hem and haw and make the process worse. The employee leaves the office miserable, not just because she has been fired, but because she didn't get a clear understanding of why. We can't stress too much how important it is for you to step up here as a leader.
4. *Make sure you deliver the termination message in a way that leaves no room for interpretation.* We know an executive who was so poor at firing people that one person didn't know he was fired. The executive called the person in to "gently" let him know that he couldn't continue working there. To everyone else's surprise, the individual showed up bright and early for work on Monday, having not understood the termination message at all because the executive talked all around the issue and never made the point clear.
5. *Give feedback all the time.* This will make Tip 3 and Tip 4 much easier. If you've been doing your job as a boss, there really shouldn't be any surprises on performance because you've been sharing with the employee the fact that there are problems and issues. This is another place where leaders shirk their duties. It's unpleasant to give someone less than positive feedback, so most just don't. Finally, the situation gets unbearable, and the bewildered employee is fired, hearing the negative feedback for the

first time. If you do this, your corner office should have bars.

6. *Be honest and be fair.* Help the employee develop an exit strategy and, most of all, help him maintain his dignity. Losing your job is ugly and stressful enough. Unless a crime has been committed, there is no reason to have to lose your dignity and sense of self-worth at the same time. As a leader, you obviously have to protect your company, but you have to protect people as well. Don't for a moment kid yourself that you aren't being judged by everyone in the company on how you do this. How and when you fire someone determines the level of respect others will give you. This is where a corporate soul mate can be invaluable, by the way.

How Not to Fire Someone

Unfortunately, the story I'm going to tell gets repeated every day across corporate America. Almost everyone knows someone who has been treated like this. A friend of mine was recently "let go" after a more than 20-year career with his company. Few people were more loyal or worked harder for the company than this individual, but the inevitable happened. The company's direction and focus changed, and the decision was made that they didn't need this employee's particular skills anymore. (*Important point:* This happens, and sometimes companies do need to make changes or transition to different skill sets. There is no issue with that.) But, instead of being thoughtful about how to celebrate that person's contributions over 20 years, and, instead of even discussing a potential exit strategy with him, the decision was made to just dismiss the employee—with no warning, no discussion. The employee was told late in the afternoon, and the office manager was waiting in the office with boxes to help him box up two decades of commitment quickly, and to escort him out of the office.

Could the employee have been given an opportunity to retire? You bet. Could there have been a going-away party? You bet. Could there have been countless other ways to have developed a creative exit strategy? You bet. Did this send a message to the entire company about the value placed on loyalty, commitment, and people? You bet!

—*Pattye*

When I Had to Fire an Entire Company

As we alluded to in our opening dialog, it's one thing to fire a person. It is another thing to fire a company. I had to do just that, and it was the hardest thing I ever did. When I left the ad agency to go to work for our largest client, I knew that I had to confront the "elephant in the room" right away. The agency was actually shrinking, and, as a result, my company was becoming a bigger and bigger part of the business. I knew I would be called on to be objective and would eventually need to conduct an agency review. I also knew that there were some when I was hired who questioned my ability and willingness to do this. So I did the only thing I could do. I was honest and upfront with my friends at the agency (and yes, they were dear friends whom I had worked with for eight years). I told them that I would have to be objective and act in the best interest of the company. I also promised them I would be fair and straightforward with them along the way.

The inevitable happened and we conducted a review. I remember a painful and tearful conversation, advising them not to waste their time pitching the business because it was very clear to us that we needed different resources than what they could provide. What made it especially painful was that the chairman of the agency decided to close the business when they lost our account. I believe and hope the employees and management team will tell you that the transition was fair and as comfortable as possible. I do know I'm still friends today with many people from the agency. The biggest lesson I learned from this is how important it is to be candid and honest. People appreciate that.

—Pattye

Just Because You Hired Them Shouldn't Mean They Can't Get Fired

Many managers in corporate America feel that if they fire someone who they were responsible for hiring, it looks bad for them. Hogwash. The only thing that looks bad is not doing something that needs to be done.

While no one hires people with the objective to turn around, in a short period of time, and fire them, mistakes do happen. You can interview extensively, and there will still be times when the fit just doesn't occur. It is important that you rid yourself of any ill-conceived bias based on who hires the individual. This is about putting together the best team you possibly can to compete in the world of business. Thinking that you can't fire someone because it will reflect poorly on you is an adolescent notion, and it has no place in the world of business.

We can't tell you how often this happens, though. As people move up the ladder, they are more and more reluctant to admit it when they make a mistake (see Instinct 13). And, there is no place where we see this more clearly than with hiring and firing. Time and again, we've counseled direct reports to hurry up and deal with a hiring mistake. Many people prefer, unfortunately, to make life miserable for an employee in hopes that he will "get the idea" and leave on his own. That way, the executives don't have to admit to anyone that they may have hired the wrong person. The reality is that the person you want to get the message rarely does, but some of your better employees do, and they will be the ones to move on.

We have one name for leaders who manage this way: cowards. It's cowardly to treat people badly so that they will leave and you don't have to fire them. Be a leader worthy of the corner office and own up to your mistakes. Obviously, you need to work with people and give them a chance to improve. You need to communicate the issues to them and objectively lay out what they must do to succeed. But, after that, do what needs to be done.

It Is Okay to Expect More from Your Friends

There is no doubt that as you start your career, you will use the workplace to form relationships. It is only natural that you will develop many friendships from your circle of work associates. After all, you spend more time at work than any place else. In the early stages of your career, odds are that you have no spouse or children at home so your social life is often derived exclusively from your friends at work. As you move up, though, you will begin to notice the roles evolving from peers to that of supervisor/direct report.

It is in the managing of friends that most people discover they are on their own. It is inevitable, yet the advice on how to handle managing friends is nowhere to be found. You won't find it outlined in any employee manual, or discussed in a round table at human resources conferences, but it goes on every day at every company in the United States.

Managing individuals with whom you have a friendship outside the office is not a problem, if managed properly and discussed openly between the two people.

As the supervisor, you will be watched closely by others to see if your friends are the recipients of special treatment. You will be watched when you interact with them versus others on your team. Once again, the key to success is to keep that company hat on at all times and to use the filter of what is in the best interest of the company and the employees. It is when that hat comes off that the trouble begins.

This scenario is especially true as you move up the corporate ladder. "Why is that?" you may ask. Well, as you become more and more responsible for hiring more senior talent, you will more than likely call on people you have worked with in your past. You will want to take fewer risks. There are risks that come with hiring an unknown versus hiring someone you have already worked with, are familiar with, and have confidence in.

The day will come when you introduce to your staff the new hire and tell them that the two of you worked together back at so-and-so. At this point, many will roll their eyes and assume the new hire has been appointed as the "fair-haired child" based merely on the fact that the two of you have a history. Because people will be people, the new kid on the block will likely receive a cold shoulder and might be left out of important meetings, or not shown the ropes. How do you deal with this?

We suggest the following ideas as some preparation and precaution in the proper managing of friends:

- Talk about it up front with both your current employees and your new hire. Assure everyone that there will be no special treatment. Do you notice a theme here? Throughout this entire chapter, we advise being candid, upfront, and honest. If there is an issue, deal with it.
- If you feel comfortable doing so, tell your friend that there *will* be special treatment. Because of your relationship, you will expect more from them—that you will expect a higher level of performance. It may not be fair, but it is the one way to avoid any criticism that you allow those who know you to provide a lower-quality work product.
- Because you socialize with a number of your direct reports, be guarded with your words regarding the office even if you are outside of a "work environment."

If you think managing friends is hard, just try managing family members. The same rules apply but are even more difficult to enforce. Even so, you must.

I Love You, But Pack Your Bags

I remember one time when I hired my daughter as a craft services manager for a convention. She did an *amazing* job. So, the next year, I hired her as a stage manager for another convention. She was such a rotten crewmember (late, lazy) that I knew I would lose control of the rest of the crew if I didn't uphold the same standard for her as for everyone else. When she was late for the third day in a row, I calmly told her that if she had read her crew manual, she would find that being late a third time was grounds for immediate dismissal. I instructed her to go pack her bags, check out of the hotel, and take a cab to the airport. She didn't speak to me for a month. But now, some seven years later, with management experience of her own, not only does she understand, she also wonders why I didn't send her home sooner.

—Dorcas Meroney, Consultant

Learn to Be Objective and You Will Always Do What Is Right

The key to this instinct is to master the ability to be objective when evaluating talent. When you can, you will have demonstrated to all that you have the character and the emotional intellect to lead—and to lead effectively.

You will never have to deal with any of the earlier situations, if you and everyone responsible for hiring always hire the right individual. If your company does nothing but grow, you will never have to implement a layoff. However, if this is your plan, might we sell you some oceanfront property in Wyoming? That's not reality, unfortunately, but this is: *you will not always hire the right person.*

There are, however, things you can do to increase the likelihood of a long-term, productive match. Here are some of the tips we've employed to augment the traditional interviewing process:

- *Have a clear and articulate statement as to the true culture of your company.* Different companies appeal to different individuals. The culture is often distinctive and clear. If the organization is extremely horizontal, with limited walls and reporting structure, a politically savvy individual from a large, overly structured environment might be a forced fit. (Oh, how we learned this the hard way!)
- *If the prospective hire is from out of town, take the time to fly to them and meet them on their home turf.* We take recruiting very seriously, and the fact that we take the time to fly to them sends an important signal. You are apt to get a truer read of the individual when he or she is on familiar ground.
- *If they are in town, talk outside the office, preferably in your home.* This creates a warm and welcoming environment, and speaks highly of how you view your employees. It will create a less structured physical environment and will serve as a catalyst for discussions outside the scope of work and more into what is really at the heart and soul of the candidate as a person.
- *If you are close to making an offer and the candidate is from out of town, bring the spouse and children into town for a weekend.* It is their weekend to explore and to get comfortable with their new home. There is nothing worse than a star hire who has a disgruntled family at home because the city is not what they thought it would be.

Conclusion

As a manager of people, your job is to put the right people in the right spots and to provide them an environment where they can exceed expectations on a daily basis.

While the rest is up to them, evaluating their performance objectively is up to you.

We recognize that this is a hard skill to learn and that some people are never good at it. If you are not good at something, you have only two choices if you want to keep advancing your cause. Get good at it, or hire a person who is, and eventually learn from him or her.

It Is a Strength to Be Able to Hire to Your Weakness

I will be the first to admit that personnel management was not one of my core strengths. I knew my weakness was not a good thing because it could prevent me, at some point, from acting in the best interest of the company. When I hired a number-two person to help me build the agency, I knew I wanted someone who would compensate for the areas I was not as strong in. It takes self-awareness and a candid self-assessment to accept where you are weak. I knew there were areas in addition to personnel management that I needed to strengthen and, by hiring Tom Millweard, my weaknesses were negated overnight. As a one-two team, we helped lead our company to record highs. I know it could not have happened had I not hired a person who was strong where I was weak.

—*Scott*

Five Questions to Ask Yourself to See if You Have the Instinct to Evaluate Talent Objectively

1. Would you be able to fire your best friend if that individual did not meet performance expectations?
2. Do you have a sense of which personality traits tend to succeed within your company culture?
3. Have you found yourself being more lenient toward underperformance by those associates with whom you have a relationship outside the office?
4. Have you asked for and received any training on the art of interviewing and firing?
5. Rather than terminating a poor performer, have you attempted to place him or her elsewhere in the company?

If you answered yes, yes, no, yes, and no, you show signs that this is an instinct that comes naturally to you.

Five Steps to Develop the Instinct to Evaluate Talent Objectively

1. Sit down with those you have a relationship with outside the office, and discuss the expectations, the challenges, and the perceptions of managing friends.
2. Conduct a talent draft. Test yourself on your ability to rank objectively your key talent, and ask yourself the question: "Would you hire them again?"

3. Implement one of our hiring practices and see if that provides you more insight into the candidate.
4. Request from HR the most current interviewing training tool they have available.
5. Examine those close to you outside of work, and observe if they are leveraging that relationship for their own benefit.

13 Oops, and Other Important Words to Lead By

SCOTT: You know, I have to hand it to you—you really are something else.

PATTYE: Why do you say that?

SCOTT: You know the whole good cop/bad cop strategy, right? Well, without my knowing it, you had me playing bad cop.

PATTYE: And just how did I do that?

SCOTT: Actually, it was a good thing, but when someone on my staff came to you, or when I admitted a mistake in front of all, you handled it with class.

PATTYE: Gee, I must apologize.

SCOTT: That's not it; you actually taught my staff, and yours, that admitting a mistake is not the end of the world. You knew that no one did it on purpose, and you expressed an expectation that it wouldn't happen again. I think because you had worked in our business, you could relate to most of the mishaps.

Pattye: Okay, I get that I'm the good cop, but how did that make you the bad cop?

Scott: Because you were so nice, I felt the need privately to play the bad cop a bit—to make sure that they understood that you would not be nearly as gracious and understanding the next time it occurred.

Pattye: So, you knew I wouldn't.

Scott: Oh, I knew all right, and I sure as hell didn't want to experience it. So there I was, playing bad cop, with the heavy hand. And they admired so much how you responded that they vowed not to disappoint you again.

Pattye: What is the name of this book—oh yeah, *Confessions.* Well, dear Scott, may I offer a confession?

Scott: Of course.

Pattye: It wasn't unplanned that you ended up playing bad cop. You forget I know you, and how you cared about the business, and how it killed you to make a mistake.

Scott: Why you . . .

Pattye: Played you just like Ringo played the drums.

Experience is simply the name we give our mistakes.
—Oscar Wilde

Make sure you can look back on your experience with pride.
—Scott and Pattye

Corner Office Instinct 13

Have the Confidence to Admit Your Mistakes and to Ask Others for Help

Shame (n.): a painful emotion caused by consciousness of guilt, shortcoming, or impropriety

Nearly one out of four employees feel their supervisors blame others to cover mistakes or minimize embarrassment according to a 2006 study by Florida State University's College of Business.

While admitting our mistakes seems to be a lesson most learned in first grade, it appears to be a foreign concept in the business world. We currently live in an interesting time when it comes to profiling corporate leadership. This is a time that undoubtedly could discourage many aspiring leaders and cause them to vow to stay clear of the corner office. Every day, they can pick up the paper and read about another deal gone bad, another attempt to hoodwink the stockholders, or, just plain cheat the system. Whether it is selling off shares of stock, falsifying documents, or having sexual relations with an intern, these scandals tend to escalate and take on a life of their own. They become major stories due to the simple fact that those involved look you right in the eye and lie: therein lies the shame. The person's first reaction is to cover it up and do anything but take responsibility for the event.

There is something inherent in many leaders that prevents them from coming clean, admitting a mistake, and moving on. It is a habit you should rid yourself of early in your career, and *never,* under any circumstances, consider it to be an alternative.

A Lesson for Life Learned the First Year on the Job

My first job was given to me by Art Casper who was one of two principals of an agency known as Winius Brandon. One of our clients was faced with a public relations emergency, and their first reaction was to cover it up. Art pushed, and pushed hard, for them to come clean and to tell it like it was. His reasoning still sticks with me today. He told them and his staff: "Never underestimate the American public's ability to forgive and forget." Some 25 years later, I realize that no truer words were ever spoken, and it is an insight that many recently sentenced corporate officials should have taken to heart. Once you admit and handle a mistake with honesty, people listen—and then they go back to getting on with their lives. It is when you dodge the truth, create an ethical misdirect, or just plain hide the truth that you are allowing the incident to continue to live, and, quite possibly, grow to proportions much larger than when it started.

—*Scott*

You *Will* Make a Mistake—Don't Make Another by How You Deal with It

In the early stages of your career, you are told repeatedly that it is never too early to begin to plan for your retirement. While that day may appear to be a long way off, it will eventually become a reality. As a result, you start to deal with it by planning and preparing. Well, we have something else you should begin to plan for: making a mistake, a screw-up, or a boo-boo that, when it surfaces, comes right around and plops in the middle of your desk, looks up at you, and says, "You did it, and everyone knows you did."

Mistakes will happen. How you handle them may very well determine the tenure and heights you will achieve in corporate America. For when that time comes, your team members, subordinates, bosses, and customers are all going to be watching how you perform in adversity. And being accountable for a mistake with all eyes on you qualifies as adversity in our book.

We are reminded of the French proverb: "Adversity creates men. Good fortune creates monsters."

This is why we say you should plan for mistakes. Make a pact with yourself that when that a mistake happens, you will step up, own it, express remorse, and promise that you will work to never make that mistake again. You should deliver your message with a conviction and confidence that leaves your associates with nothing other than respect for your character.

Practice saying these four powerful words: "I made a mistake."

If you have direct reports, you should also begin to think about your reaction when one of your employees makes a mistake. That is equally important because everyone else in your organization will be watching you when that happens as well. Your reaction to a mistake will set the tone for risk. If someone is raked over the coals, you can bet the message you are sending to everyone is to play it safe. Playing it safe usually translates into no innovations, no breakthroughs, and no big ideas. If you have created a learning organization, mistakes are treated as important learning. The tone and result are up to you.

When a Killer Coupon Was a Killer

A junior account executive who handled a food account came into my office and informed me of a mistake. It seems that a "Buy One, Get One" coupon (which is a loss leader) for a restaurant was supposed to be *one* of four coupons in a citywide drop, but instead mistakenly made up *two* of the four coupons. It was too late to change it because it was already produced and in the mail. I called an emergency meeting of the franchisee board to inform the operators. I said there was no excuse for it, it was our fault, and we would compensate them for what they felt the wrong coupon would cost them. Their reaction was something I will never forget. They said they appreciated us coming forward, offering no excuse, and while the offer we made was generous, they couldn't accept it. Privately, I was told they were impressed that we chose not to name names and throw any of our employees under the bus. That taught me that it is possible for mistakes to actually serve as the catalyst for making relationships stronger—but only if handled properly.

—*Scott*

We are reminded that many of the instincts that helped us reach the corner office are also solid instincts that help govern how you conduct your life outside of work.

The most important thing to any of us should be our character. How we deal with adversity provides the truest test of our character. It is in the face of adversity that we find out what kind of leaders we will eventually become. There is a high road and a low road: Which will you take?

If You Think Asking for Help Is a Sign of Weakness, Think Again

"Can you help me?" are four other very powerful words. They will greatly influence how others view you, and the speed at which you will learn. People who think admitting to a mistake is a black mark on their professional record probably also think that asking for help shows a lack of intellect and will be perceived as a sign of weakness. We have noticed repeatedly that as people move up the corporate ladder, for some reason, they find it more and more difficult to ask for help. It shouldn't be that way, but it is.

We think that the willingness to ask for help is actually a true demonstration of humility. Quite frankly, we believe that too few leaders *still* have enough of this character trait.

Notice that we emphasized the word *still.* It is our contention that most leaders (not all) have humility early on. They start their careers by operating on the ethical high ground. If a mistake is made, they will admit it and ask for help—a trait they see as a sign of curiosity and a willingness to learn.

Yet, as the promotions pile up, this ethical foundation begins to get chipped away and starts to erode. The stakes become higher, and the willingness to admit a mistake is weighed against the pros of keeping quiet. And, as the titles and salary increases, we are less willing to say, "I need some help."

We all know the running joke about how men won't ever stop and ask for directions, regardless of how lost they are. If this myth is true, how hard do you think it would be to get the same men to ask for help? It is important to dispel the notion that admitting to a mistake or asking for help somehow demonstrates a weakness—for men or women. To the contrary, asking for help shows an ability to understand the situation and needs to be done to move on.

So, why does this guy [who will remain unnamed] keep driving even when he knows he is lost? His girlfriend has been begging him to stop for miles and ask for help. He knows if he finds his destination, it will only be by luck, and, more likely than not, he will just end up driving aimlessly, wasting a lot of time, and finally having to ask for directions. The reason he doesn't stop can be found in his motivation, and his motivation is to *impress* his girlfriend. The same motivation is there for the up-and-coming executive—to *impress* the boss.

This is a crucial point. Turn off your phone, lock the front door, gather the children around this book, and read the following out loud for all to hear:

> You impress no one when you waste everyone's time and energy by *hoping* to deliver what is expected of you. The decision to not ask for help at the point where you know you are either physically or intellectually lost is one of the worst decisions you can make. In the end, other people will think you are an ass and your bosses will doubt your ability to assess a situation and conclude that you have an inability to manage your resources.

The irony of it all is that most people love to help and share what they know. Frequently, they are flattered that, by asking for their help, you have demonstrated a high level of confidence in them, and you have shown that you value their opinion and insight.

The most important aspect of asking for help is what it says about you. It demonstrates to those above and below you that you don't expect to have all the answers, that you have enough confidence to reach out to others for help, and that you have a strong sense of what is needed to accurately complete a project.

You might be surprised at how willing those in senior management are to help and advise anyone who will ask. Most love to talk about their journey, their company, the industry, and the area of expertise that has helped them rise to the top. By asking for their help or insight, you are merely tapping into already existing "parental nurturing." Most people who have made it to the top rungs of the corporate ladder are thrilled to share the insights they have gathered and are flattered to be asked to mentor a young and curious mind. That's a far cry from the black mark many associate with asking for help.

How Does the Company Make Money?

I think I learned to ask for help and to ask questions because of my journalism training. I can't tell you how valuable two things have been to my career—the willingness to ask for help, and the ability to admit I don't understand something. One time in particular stands out. The CFO of the company was always at odds with what marketing was attempting to do. I truly didn't understand his constant objections, so I finally went to him and asked for help. I asked if he would spend some time helping me understand how the company makes money and what his concerns were. He was delighted to have a student and spent a great deal of time teaching me. It was time well spent because I learned the economics of the business. That made me a better employee, and it allowed me to be better prepared—either with programs that alleviated concerns, or to be able to address negative comments. To this day, the one piece of advice I give young people is to ask the CFO of their company to explain how the business makes money.

—*Pattye*

You should not only look up the corporate ladder in asking for help, but down and across as well. The words "can you help me?" carry with them a powerful request for dependence on another human being—to many the most gratifying thing they can do is to help someone else. If you ask one of your peers, or even one of your direct reports for help, you will be amazed at the reaction. Everyone knows something you don't. Making it to the corner office is a reflection of how well you use your resources as well as your ability to seek out, retain, and grow your base of knowledge. Asking for help is a great tool to do just that.

Even Competitors Will Help

Jim Day, recently retired chairman and CEO of Noble Corp., discovered early in his career that even competitors like to be asked for help and to share their insights. Day assumed the leadership role at Noble in his late 30s during one of the most depressed periods in the oil and gas industry's history in the United States. At that time, Noble Corp. had 350 offshore personnel.

> Jim made appointments with the CEOs of the major companies in the drilling business to ask them where they thought the energy business was headed and to gain any other insights he could. Jim says that competitors were surprisingly candid and that it helped him understand the issues better and formulate strategies. But Jim didn't stop there. In those very lean years, he turned to his employees and asked for their help in making critical decisions about cutting salaries or eliminating positions. He continued that practice of asking for help during his 24 years at the helm, and it has served him, and the company, well. Today, Noble Corp. is an $11 billion industry leader with over 6,000 offshore personnel.
>
> —*Pattye*

So, the next time you are lost, are you going to ask for directions?

One Other Question to Use Often on Your Way to the Corner Office

We have one other question that we strongly ask you to consider as a permanent part of your corporate persona. This will be especially helpful as you begin to move up and increase your number of direct reports.

What Are Your Thoughts?

We have found that when you are the senior person in a meeting that most employees go into the meeting pretty much expecting the solution to come out of your mouth as some revelation. While, on occasion this may be true, the fact is that even Babe Ruth made an out nearly 7 of every 10 times he went to the plate.

Meetings should have an inherent operating philosophy that *all will contribute.* If you think about it, what is the point of gathering people in a room to discuss something if only three of the eight attendees participate? One of our pet peeves is the "professional, go-to-a-meeting-but-never-speak-a-word" middle managers. These managers walk out with a look of accomplishment when all they did was sit there. We encourage you to rid your staff of those who view meetings as a spectator sport rather than a participation sport. At some point in the meeting, ask, "What are your thoughts?" Go around the room and, remember, don't judge, just listen, and ask others what they think of the idea brought forth.

Two things will happen. First, you will begin to see what talented people you have and how they think. This will help guide who you begin to groom and mentor for the next phase. Second, your attendees will start to become solution-focused and will begin to strategize how they prepare for the meetings. Word will get around how you "do" your meetings. This process will serve to accelerate the problem-solving abilities of your staff. After all, that is one of the many things a strong and effective leader should do.

Conclusion

What do all of these four-word phrases have to do with making it to the corner office? Everything.

You will be tested often throughout your career. How you respond to mistakes—yours or others—will demonstrate your leadership abilities in times of adversity.

How often you reach out to others for help and for their opinions will demonstrate your ability to lead people.

Be honest, be forthcoming, ask for help, and own up to your responsibility. It may be painful—but to those with dreams of reaching the corner office, there is no alternative.

Five Questions to Ask Yourself to See if You Have the Instinct of Confidence

1. Have you ever stood up in front of your team or boss and said, "I made a mistake"?
2. Have you ever gone to your boss, or someone senior, and asked them for help on something you should know but don't?
3. Did you ever try to cover up a problem in hopes it would never be discovered?
4. Have you ever asked someone who reports to you for help?
5. Have you ever voluntarily given credit to those from whom you asked for help?

If you answered yes, yes, no, yes, and yes, you have the makings of a humble leader. If you didn't, we suggest you jump off your pedestal before you get pushed off.

Five Steps to Develop the Instinct of Confidence

1. Have a "personal mistake" plan in place so you will have no questions about how you will respond when the inevitable—a mistake—happens.
2. Become a student of corporate America's leaders who are in the news and watch how they respond to adversity.

3. At your very next meeting, kick things off with the question: "What do you think?"
4. As you move up the ladder, make it a point to ask those who report to you for help on an issue crucial either to you or to the company.
5. Start applying these practices in your everyday life—and it will become effortless at work.

14 If They Give It, Take It: Take All of It

Scott: It's okay for an instinct or two to be things we discovered later in our careers, isn't it?

Pattye: Of course. We couldn't have gotten everything right from the time of birth.

Scott: Well, we could have, but, hey, that is another book. I sense that you were like me when it came to taking vacation time—in a word, horrible?

Pattye: Depends on how you define vacation—you won't find my definition in *Webster's.* But, yes, I was bad. For the longest time, my kids thought that a convention badge was a part of their family vacation.

Scott: That's bad, but it is still time away. I played the game of taking a Monday off and calling a three-day weekend a vacation. To top it off, I called in to the office to see how things were going. What an idiot I was.

Pattye: I called in, too. I could change from vacation personality to president personality in record time if I heard about something that was going wrong.

Scott: We were two leaders who did not know how to get away.

Pattye: Correct me if I'm wrong, but weren't you always preaching to your employees about taking all their time off and that it was their right to use up their vacation time?

Scott: Yeah, I know, but you have heard the saying "Do as I say, not as I do"? Vacation was a perfect example of that.

Pattye: Something tells me that may not have been the only "do as I say" example.

Scott: Now, play nice.

I travel not to go anywhere, but to go. I travel for travels' sake. The great affair is to move.

—Robert Louis Stevenson

To move and to travel is to clear your mind from work, and to replace work with an appreciation of the journey.

—Scott and Pattye

Corner Office Instinct 14

Recharging and Reenergizing Is a Requirement

Recharge (v.): to refresh, restore: revitalize

According to the fourth annual survey by Expedia.com, at least 30 percent of employed adults gave up vacation time they earned. This results in Americans handing back to their employers 415 million vacation days. On average, the typical employed American handed back three days of vacation, up 50 percent in 2003.

Why do so many workers have a problem utilizing their vacation time year after year?

In most cases, there is a company willing to pay emloyees for taking time off, and in far too many cases, the time goes unused. When you read that out loud, it sounds preposterous.

Who would not take advantage of this? What logical reason could a person have, other than claiming insanity, not to take paid vacation days? What's more insane is when you hear people voluntarily saying, "It's too much trouble. I would rather stay at the office."

We hear all the talk and statistics about how we Americans work more hours than our counterparts in most other countries, but the sad truth is we do little to give ourselves a break from it. We recently read a study that reports nearly one in five workers say they work through their lunch every day while a total of

62 percent admit they work through lunch at least once a week. When you couple the work hours with the reluctance to take vacation time, the toll on the human spirit is quite predictable: burnout. It is frustrating to watch a star performer slowly burn out, lose patience, and begin to display poor judgment as a byproduct of not getting away and clearing his or her head. This is a self-inflicted wound that can be easily prevented.

We hope you develop this instinct at the earliest possible point in your career. If not, it will eventually catch up to you (trust us on this one).

As discussed in the opening dialogue, this was an instinct we did not value as much as we should have. We were both horrible at taking time off, and when we did, we were not really gone. Most years, we worked until we got sick, and then our time away from the office was recovering from some illness. Guess we were slow on taking that as a sign, a hint that both of us were merely human, and that burnout knows no boundaries. The irony is that we'd preach the power of disengaging from work until we were blue in the face; however, our inability to apply it to our own lives played a major role in both of us walking away from our dream jobs in just our mid-40s.

Looking back now, all we can say is, "What the heck were we thinking?" For those of you reading this book, start embracing the power that comes from recharging and reenergizing your mind. We ask you to view recharging as a nonnegotiable job requirement.

There was a Method to His Madness

I worked for a man who traveled with his freinds or his family to places most of us have never heard of. They were dropped in some out-of-the-way location and spent a week fishing, camping, or whatever one does in the remote outskirts of civilization. It never sounded all that interesting to me, but, upon reflection, I remember one other aspect of his itinerary—there was no way to get in touch with him. Odd, I first thought. Brilliant, I now think. We had to take care of our business before he left. After all, it was only one week, so we most certainly could manage. Oh, to be away and out of touch from the office. It must have felt like one month. As I said—brilliant.

—*Scott*

It Is Not So Much Where You Go, but Rather What You Do, or Don't Do, with Your Time

The Irreplaceable Syndrome

One of the classic reasons people don't take time off is because they live in a world of inflated self-importance. We don't say this to be mean, but many times we have asked different employees about taking time off, only to have the response be one of the following (and, to be fair, it's probably been our response many times also):

- I will think about it when we get through the planning process next month. *I need* to be here.
- I will think about it after the big meeting in three weeks. *I need* to be at the meeting.
- I will, but there is just so much on my plate right now. *I need* to get through the next project.

- I would, but I don't have anyone to cover for me right now. *I need* to make sure the work gets done.
- I have something on my calendar every week through this quarter. *I need* to be at each meeting.

Everyone is probably too liberal with the use of the word *need.* Here is a newsflash: There will always be meetings or something on the calendar, so what you really need to do is prioritize. If you plan ahead, missing a meeting will not be a major catastrophe—you can communicate what needs to be done to those who are covering for you. If the company will suffer from your absence for a week, there are some bigger issues that must be resolved.

We know there are some who believe that by not taking their vacation time, they are sending a message to their supervisors about their commitment and work ethic. Some probably believe it to be a sign of weakness to use all the vacation time allotted them. For those who think like this, get the name of a good therapist and pick up the phone because you need help. The only message this sends to your supervisors is that you place little, if any, value on your mental health. In reality, not taking time off merely demonstrates a lack of sound and responsible judgment.

We encourage you at the start of the year to plan your time off and block it on your calendar just as you would a business trip. Take that pen and draw a line through an entire week, and if you have earned it, find another week and do the same. Don't worry about what you will do on vacation. We want you to feel how liberating it is to declare, at the start of the year, when your time off will be. Write in big letters RECHARGE WEEK. When you begin to focus on the benefits, you will be more likely to make it happen.

If you don't plan for it, another year will get away from you, but, more important, you won't ever get a second chance to live that year over.

A Tough Lesson

Many years ago, after I had moved away from San Diego, my best friend Chris Franklin set up a trip for four friends, including me, to go to Hawaii on a trip that coincided with a big meeting. I was in charge of the advertising for a local franchise group, and they met once a month to discuss their advertising. I half-heartedly booked a flight from Houston to Hawaii, but, as the date drew closer, I talked myself into *not* being able to miss the monthly meeting of the franchise group. I created some importance around an issue that today I can't even remember. I thought I was acting in the best interest of the company. I had to attend this meeting.

As a result, I ate the ticket and did not go on the trip. The monthly meeting was just like all others. But, months later, I received a phone call at 2:00 A.M., notifying me that my best friend Chris had dropped dead in front of his house after a run—his heart had stopped. After returning from the funeral, I took that unused ticket and had it framed. I put it close to me in whatever office I occupied. It was there to remind me to value the opportunity to take time away, and that it's only when we take time away from the office that we are able to begin a journey with others. The ticket was there to also remind me to never cancel a trip. There isn't much I wouldn't give today to have seven more days of memories with Chris. But there are no do-overs.

—Scott

What Are You Waiting For? Grab Your Calendar

But I Have Nowhere to Go

Another barrier to not utilizing your vacation time is the "I don't really have anywhere to go" syndrome. Our first response is "Who says you have to go anywhere?" To be effective, this instinct does not require you to fly a minimum number of miles or create a mandatory two-time-zone separation from the office. Instead, this instinct is about disengaging from work and clearing your mind for the next six-month sprint. It is easy to disengage and come back recharged even if you opt to stay at home.

Many are hesitant to take vacation time to stay at home because it is, after all, called "vacation time." Companies who refer to the time away as vacation days are doing their employees a disservice. People think of vacation as travel, and, if there is no travel planned: well, it just seems odd. We would like the days to be called time-off days, recharge days, no work days—anything that more closely aligns with the ultimate benefit. We believe that if employees had 10 "recharge" days, they would have no problem using them. If staying at home and watching television was all they wanted to do, they could take the time off to do it.

If you find yourself with no cruise or trip planned and have blocked a week off, don't give it back. Instead, let us offer some suggestions for ways to have a great recharge week:

- Make a list of the five things you have wanted to do to your house and have never gotten around to. By the end of the week, accomplish three of them.
- Hold your own movie festival. Each day, pick out an early afternoon movie and catch up on all the films you said you wanted to see.
- Schedule lunches and dinners with friends who you have neglected or have had difficulty seeing.
- Tackle the closet; take everything you have not worn in the past year and donate it to a charity of your choice. While you are at it, tackle the garage and throw out some of that junk.
- Sleep late; stay up late. Have a reading day, television day, explore day, clean day—you get the idea.

We guarantee you will come back more reenergized than if you traveled somewhere and got back the day before you return to work.

Now Go Grab That Movie Section

It is Never Too Late to Learn This Instinct

One of my closest friends, Ed Johnson, is a world-class interior landscaper. He is responsible for the interior landscaping of some of the wealthiest and biggest names in San Diego. Yet, Ed has probably never used all his time off in any year that I have known him (except for a two-week recovery from hernia surgery, which I have reiterated to him does not really count as time off to recharge). When he takes any time, it is around a home improvement project. This year, he had a mural he was going to work on and scheduled a week off. The project fell through, but Ed still took the week off and, in his words, his eyes were opened. He spent the week thinking about one thing—himself. He slept late, went to the gym when he wanted, caught a movie, and basically decompressed. His revelation was "Why have I not been doing this all along?" If that project hadn't fallen through, Ed would still be operating in the world of "I'll take time off when I have a commitment I need to see to." As we talk about time off next year, Ed, at the spry young age of 51, realizes that there is now a commitment every year to recharge.

—*Scott*

We Don't Want to Hear from You

Others might differ with our take on this, but we believe when you embrace this instinct, you also embrace the notion that a key part of recharging is dependent on your ability to stay away from anything office related. We feel strongly that this is a zero-tolerance issue. We also realize that it's time for a disclaimer: We didn't practice this, or do enough to encourage others to practice this, but, with what we know now, we wish we had.

When you take your days off, do not call in or check e-mail. Instead, clear your mind. If you check e-mails or call in every day, you are tempting fate. You are putting yourself in a situation to get sucked into work issues that put you emotionally and intellectually right back at the office.

Splish, Splash! It's a Conference Call

A number of years ago, I was on "vacation" at Disneyworld with my young daughter, but I was really trying to juggle vacation and work, checking e-mails every morning and night, sandwiching in conference calls between visits to theme parks. But I convinced myself I was handling it all.

One afternoon I hit a major conflict. A conference call was scheduled at the last minute that I just had to attend, but I had promised my daughter we would go to the pool. I thought the call would be short, so I figured I could juggle both. We headed to the pool and settled down in our chairs—far away from the noise and the pool. I told my daughter I'd get off quickly, and then we'd swim. But, the call droned on—my daughter was getting hot and cranky, so we moved closer to the pool so she could swim and I could talk and keep an eye on her (this was before cell phones had mute buttons).

I hadn't confessed to my colleagues that I was at the pool, or that I was doing anything more important than talking to them. Soon, someone said, "What's that noise—it sounds like water and splashing?" At a pool at Disneyworld, there *is* a lot of splashing and there *are* a lot of kids. To muffle the noise, I wrapped my towel around my head and the cell phone. That helped, but I was starting to sweat. Boy, was it hot inside that towel. One towel had to become two—I could barely see. I had just enough of an opening to watch my little girl. But, I was getting hotter and hotter. I finally got my daughter's attention and had her take my empty water bottle and fill it up. For the next half hour, she filled up my water bottle, and I poured it on my head and the rest of my body to ward off heat stroke. But I finished the call, and that was the important thing, right?

—*Pattye*

What makes getting away even more difficult is the fact that more and more people have a PDA as their cell phone, which means they are taking their e-mails with them. All we can say is, don't do it—turn the e-mail part *off,* and don't look at it. If needed, and you are traveling with someone else, use their cell phone to avoid the temptation. Figure out how you are going to handle this before you embark on your time off. Unfortunately, this is the new reality. It is imperative that you not let technology invade and potentially influence your ability to disengage. You never know which e-mail will take you out of the "away mode" and zap you right back into that "work frame of mind" that you so desperately need to avoid.

Leave Ego and Technology at Home

I have two daughters—10 years apart. As I reflect back on how I took "mom-and-daughter" trips with both of them, I realize what a difference 10 years made in how we vacationed. Ego and technology played a big role in that difference. I took Melissa with me on a number of business trips, often for the Arthritis Foundation. I'd only have a couple of days of meetings, and then we spent the rest of the week exploring the area—Washington, DC; Florida; and some great places.

I wasn't so important, and I didn't have the technology to constantly check in, so we truly had vacation time. She also got to attend some meetings and see what her mom did, which is healthy. Fast-forward 10 years. I took the same type of trips with my second daughter, Lindsey. We had meetings at the beginning, and then we would go explore. There was one huge difference. I was much more important (in my own mind), so I constantly checked messages on my BlackBerry; one inevitably would cause me to call the office and move to work mode. I also answered my cell phone, which meant Lindsey had to patiently wait for me to finish a phone call. It was so unnecessary and so unfair to her.

—*Pattye*

Conclusion

This instinct is not easy. We understand all too well how hard it is to disengage, but we also understand all too well how critical it is to do so. Mastering this instinct requires planning and exceptional communications prior to your time off. It will be worth it. If you make this a nonnegotiable clause in your yearly contract with yourself, you will be healthier, happier, and have a longer, more productive career.

Five Questions to Ask Yourself to See if You Have the Instinct to Recharge and Reenergize

1. Do you ever have unused days off at the end of the year?
2. Do you feel the need to travel during your time off?
3. Do you encourage those who report to you to take time off?

4. Do you look at those who use up all their days off and feel some resentment?
5. Have you ever cancelled days off in an attempt to show your bosses how important work is to you?

If you answered no, no, yes, no, and no, we salute you. We also wish we had had your perspective throughout our careers.

Five Steps to Develop the Instinct of Recharge and Reenergize

1. Go to your calendar right now and block out the remaining days off you have.
2. Schedule a quick single day off. Just hang out around town and don't call in. This will be a test to prove to you that the world at work will continue to operate.
3. Require your direct reports to give you their scheduled time off for the year by January 15. Begin to view it as an expectation and a part of their annual objectives.
4. In lieu of other perks, award additional days off. The cost is less and the upside to the company is a reenergized employee.
5. Do not take your PDA with you on any personal travel.

15 Honey, When Did We Have a Third Child?

Scott: Since this is the last chapter, it's time to truly confess.

Pattye: You go first.

Scott: Okay. In our book, we've identified 15 instincts that we believe are important to practice and to live by if you want to succeed and make it to the corner office. And, I think we would give ourselves an A, or an A+, on 13 of those instincts. There's no doubt that they helped get us to the corner office. But . . .

Pattye: Okay, I can finish the sentence. But, we'd both give ourselves a D on Instinct 14 and an F on Instinct 15.

Scott: As hard as it is to admit, I agree. We were not good at taking time off (Instinct 14), and we were so totally work-obsessed for much of our careers that we truly neglected our friends and family (Instinct 15).

Pattye: You know what's ironic about this? I remember that both of us really worked hard to get our team members to take vacation time and to make family time.

Scott: I have another word for it—but I'll keep it to myself. I guess we were the poster children for "Do as we say, not as we do." Here's an important question for you: Do you think you would have still made it to the corner office if you had worked harder at making your family a priority?

Pattye: Knowing what I know now—absolutely. There are plenty of executives out there who have figured out how to balance their priorities. I wasn't one of them. Here's a question for you: Would you have become chairman if you had taken a vacation?

Scott: Duh, somehow I think I could have swung it. I can tell you what else would have happened if we had both taken real vacations and made our personal lives a priority—we wouldn't have burned out and walked away from our careers in our mid-40s.

Pattye: You know what I think? For a long stay in the corner office, this may be our most powerful instinct of all.

Time is the coin of your life. It is the only coin you have, and only you can determine how it will be spent. Be careful lest you let other people spend it for you.

—Carl Sandburg

You have a limited number of coins (time). Spend them wisely on true priorities.

—Scott and Pattye

Corner Office Instinct 15

Make Your Personal Life a Priority

Priority (n.): to be treated as more important than somebody or something else

A recent study commissioned by Lexmark International found that 92 percent of respondents say they make or take work-related communications outside of work, including on vacations. Nearly three-fourths say they stay "switched on" during weekends and a fifth of them have interrupted a date for work purposes.

The facts speak for themselves. We are certain this survey by Lexmark International is merely scratching the surface. The once visible separation of work life and personal life is now becoming more and more blurred. While many seek work/life balance, research by executive consulting firm RHR International suggests that companies do not prepare their managers adequately to communicate the right, balanced message to future leaders or to engage in dialogue with them about their career interests, family and personal needs, and other issues related to assuming more significant responsibilities.

As you move up the ladder, it takes even more self-monitoring and effort to ensure that you balance career with family and personal needs, but that topic is rarely discussed. We think we talked about the importance of balance to our employees, but we certainly didn't "walk the talk." We did just the opposite. We failed miserably at making our personal lives a priority.

This is the real confession. Two former corporate leaders are willing to tell everyone that we failed at living this instinct, but you don't have to fail. We both agree that this is our biggest regret as we reflect back on our careers. We shudder to think how much worse it would have been if we had been wired with BlackBerries and cell phones at the very beginning of our careers instead of just getting them in the past decade.

That's why this chapter is so important. As a matter of fact, when we first sat down to write a book about our experiences, almost the entire focus was on warning those entering or already in the workforce that they must find a way to create balance. Without balance, you will eventually be of little use to anyone, including yourself. Even though this is the final instinct in the book, do not assume that it is the least important. To the contrary, our failure to make good on this instinct is one of the major reasons we left our positions. We put our jobs and our career paths above everything else. The irony is that nowhere is that an expectation of, or a requirement for, reaching the corner office. We were blessed that we were able to walk away at a young age and start the slow process of reclaiming so much of what we ignored. Few will be in such a position, so it is crucial that this instinct be developed and practiced early on.

We doubt anyone would disagree with the statement that you need to find a way to balance your personal life with your work life. Everyone agrees with that, but it's darn hard to do when you're trying to climb that corporate ladder.

Plus, in earlier chapters, we told you that you have to have a passionate love affair with the office and that *9 to 5* was just a movie. We also told you to take your nutcracker with you everywhere you go.

So, what do we want you to do here? First, understand these instincts do not *all* get developed at the same time, and once developed, they do not require the same level of human capital (known as time) to maintain. When properly developed and nurtured, these instincts become second nature in guiding your leadership style. And once they become second nature, the opportunity to create balance exists. Recognize this opportunity and seize it. We didn't, and we'll regret it forever.

It's so easy to fall into the trap of working all the time, believing that you are indispensable, and becoming addicted to your technology and being always connected. After all, many of the role models you see—like us—are doing just that. Even though we wanted our staff to take time off for family events and pushed them to take vacations (in one case, we even took an employee and his wife to dinner and gave them an expense-paid trip to Mexico because he never took vacation), we chose not to model that behavior. We could have, and we should have. As we look back, we would have been healthier, happier, and, quite probably, more productive as a result if we had made time for friends, family, and vacations. We certainly would not have burned out so early.

My Baby Left Me a Voice Mail

One evening when our second daughter, Lindsey, was about three months old, I was still at work later than I should have been. As I was packing up to finally go home, I noticed I had a voice mail waiting. Since it could be something "important," I stopped to listen to it. All that was on the message was a baby crying: my baby. It was a subtle message from my dear, patient husband who must have been at the end of his rope. Quite honestly, it was too subtle for me to get.

—*Pattye*

We have come to realize that making time for your personal life—whether it's your faith, friends, family, hobbies, or exercise—is an instinct that can be developed, nurtured, and honed just like the others. In retrospect, we wish someone had given us permission, or pushed us, to better nurture this instinct.

Who Has Time for Friends?

I was blessed with wonderful friends every place I moved, but I was saddened one night when I was going through pictures. I sat on the floor and cried. I realized that when I moved for a new job, I spent zero energy reaching back to my friends to remain a part of their lives. I just couldn't find the time. I stand corrected: I chose not to find the time. My tears were for the fact that these photos were all I had left of many promising friendships. With just a minimum of effort, I could have been the richest man in the world. Unfortunately, I never saw the treasures these wonderful people could have added to my life, even after I moved away from them.

—*Scott*

This is our gift to you. We want you to know that you *can* make time for your personal life *and* make it to the corner office. We want you to know you have permission to do so.

Think of Your Family as Your Biggest Client

The reality is your family is your biggest client. Losing big clients or customers can be devastating to your company. Going through a divorce or missing your kids growing up is even more devastating.

When You're at the Game, Be at the Game

I really tried hard to juggle the many demands of being a working mom, and was constantly rationalizing that multitasking was the solution to everything. I tried to make as many of my daughter's soccer games as possible, even if I really needed to be on a conference call at the same time. I would attend a game and stand behind the bleachers talking on the conference call and trying to watch the game—at least that's what I told myself. Somehow, though, I managed to miss the important plays—the goal or the pass she made. But I wasn't alone. Sometimes there wasn't enough room behind the stands for all the parents who needed to be on phone calls—but we were at the game, weren't we? No, not really. It hurts that I can't get those games back.

—*Pattye*

You Live Where Now?

With moving so much, I think I got used to the idea that family was not going to be an integral part of my life. If I was to make it big in my chosen industry, it would be me that would make it happen, and only me. I decided I had little time for the extras. Because I had three brothers and parents in four different locations, I needed to pick and choose. My parents and one brother got my travel time. How short-sighted I was, and how I shortchanged myself. There are nephews and nieces I have not even seen. There are houses and towns where my brothers have lived for years that I have not visited. This may be my single greatest regret as I reflect on the journey to the top.

—Scott

To keep those big clients, it's typical to go to any lengths to nurture the relationship. What would happen if you applied the same energy and creativity to your family? We believe you might be surprised what would happen if you applied that kind of discipline to your personal relationships. Here are some examples we found from people who do a good job at this:

- *Schedule your kids' games.* Sit down with your kids, explain your work, and work out compromises. Explain that you can't come to every game, but that you can come to the ones that you schedule. Then keep your word.
- *Plan for anniversaries, birthdays, and other special occasions as if they were presentations to the board.* Would you have your assistant throw together a PowerPoint presentation the day of the meeting? Of course not, but you'd have her run out and buy a card or send flowers the day of your anniversary. Stop that. Plan for those special occasions well in advance and orchestrate dinner, theatre, and parties, as if the event were for your most important client. Guess what? It is.
- *Schedule date nights with your spouse or significant other.* We really admire the couples who have a date night once a

week—even after 25 or 30 years of marriage. They get it. We didn't.

- *Connect your kids to your travel.* Whenever I (Pattye) had to be out of town for several days, I hid small gifts (gum, mints, nail polish) for the girls, and I left them an envelope for each day with a clue. That night, we talked about their scavenger hunt and their gifts. It's true some might see this as a way to "pay" for my guilt of being gone. It was, but it also kept me connected and let the girls know I was thinking about them.

We used family as the example. That doesn't mean that if you're single, you should work all the time. Apply these same principles to your friends, your hobbies, and even your exercise program.

Conclusion

We know that careers are demanding, and that there will be inevitable events or issues that will require you to work long hours—a new business presentation, a merger, or an acquisition. We know you will have demanding bosses who will expect you to be there all the time. We know you will be competing with colleagues who are eager to show that they are always at work and the first to respond. We know that you can't achieve balance every single day. We also know that you can choose to achieve balance overall if you work at it as hard as you work at work. Most companies and most leaders look to promote other leaders who have balance in their lives. We didn't punish those folks who had a life outside of work. We encouraged it.

Always remember, you have a choice. Make the right one as often as you can. We wish we had more often.

Five Questions to Ask Yourself to See if You Have the Instinct of Making Your Personal Life a Priority

1. Have you repeatedly missed your kids' games, concerts, or events?
2. Do you take all of your vacation time, and we really mean take it—without taking conference calls, using your BlackBerries, and answering voice mail.
3. Can your friends count on you to show up at events and not cancel all the time?
4. Do you have a hobby, or do you work out regularly?
5. Have you ever rationalized being out of town on an important occasion like a birthday or anniversary—saying we can celebrate later?

If you answered no, yes, yes, yes, no, congratulations! You have a life. And, yes, you can still get to the corner office.

Five Steps You Can Take to Begin Developing the Instinct of Making Your Personal Life a Priority

1. Put that BlackBerry to good use. Stop what you're doing, and enter birthdays, anniversaries, spring breaks, and all other important family dates. Block them out. For celebrations, block time now on your calendar to shop and plan in advance. If it's scheduled, it will get done.
2. Set aside special family time each day when you are not reachable. Turn all your devices off, and devote your full attention to your family.
3. Treat scheduled family time and events like board meetings and presentations. Don't be late. Schedule enough time so you will be on time. This is a big deal.

4. Be spontaneous. Come home from work unexpectedly; show up at a child's school with lunch by surprise. Call friends and invite them to dinner. We realize you may have to schedule this spontaneity, but surprise them.
5. When you are present, be present. Watching a movie with your briefcase and laptop is not considered being present by most friends, spouses, and, certainly not by children. We speak from experience.

From the Authors

We've shared our stories, both good and bad, regarding the 15 instincts. Now, it's your turn. We would like you to share your stories about how you have personally put these instincts into action. Also, feel free to share stories (much like we have) that demonstrate some managers just don't get it and probably never will. We don't need to know names, but often you learn as much from the bad as you do the good.

Email us at: **Scott.aylward@gmail.com** or **Pattyemoore @gmail.com.**

Index

N

O

P

Q

R

S

T

U

V

W